WAR BONDS

by
Jack Goldman

Zorba Press
Ithaca, New York

War Bonds. Copyright © 2025 by Jack Richard Goldman. All rights reserved. Except for brief excerpts in reviews, no part of this work may be reproduced without express permission from the publisher.

Printed in the United States of America. First printing 2025.

Editing and Book design by Zorba Editing in Ithaca, New York.

ISBN (paperback): 9780927379724

Daniel Berrigan photo by Thomas Good. Creative Commons license
https://creativecommons.org/licenses/by-sa/4.0/deed.en
https://commons.wikimedia.org/wiki/File:NLN_Dan_Berrigan.jpg

Atomic bomb photo:
https://commons.wikimedia.org/wiki/File:Nagasakibomb.jpg

The lines on page 171 are from the song "I Never Was" by Linda Hirschhorn. The original source for this song is the website Recustom.com. The lyrics are inspired by the well-known "First they came..." poem by Pastor Martin Niemöller.
https://www.recustom.com/clips/i-never-was-song-by-linda-hirschhorn-4064666

Front cover image: the painting "Unencompassed", by Barbara Mink. Back cover author photo by Sheryl Sinkow.

ZP Printing code: Inside 019. Cover 003.

Published by Zorba Press
in Ithaca, New York, USA
https://ZorbaPress.com

For permissions or bulk orders, contact the publisher:
books@zorbapress.com

Chapter 1

There is an old snapshot of me taken when I was about five years old. I am dressed in a blue and white sailor boy outfit with short pants, and I am standing in the doorway of my grandfather's delicatessen store in the Bronx. My curly hair is still baby blonde, and I am staring directly at the camera. In the window on my right is the family name GOLDMAN'S and on my left is the word NUTS. It's likely that my father, Georgie as he was called, had taken the photo to annoy my grandfather, against whose Orthodox practices he had rebelled at an early age. This assumption of mine is based on another photo my father took on the occasion of my 13th birthday, after we had moved to California. I am dressed in the traditional garb of a Jewish boy at his bar mitzvah: dark suit, fringed prayer shawl, and a white yarmulke. Apparently, the formal ceremony is over because I am shown smiling and cutting a slice of cake. What is not evident is that there had been no bar mitzvah at all. The scene had been staged by my father who took the photo with a Brownie reflex camera in our backyard patio. Several weeks before, a box had arrived from my grandfather with a letter saying that the enclosed garments were for me to wear at my bar mitzvah and that he would like pictures of this important event. My father put the glossy prints in a manila envelope addressed to my grandfather and asked me to write a note thanking him. As he licked the envelope, he winked at me: "Now you are a man," he said.

My father had dropped out of school in the 5th grade. Unlike his three sisters and two brothers, he refused to work in the family delicatessen. He openly scoffed at my grandfather's Orthodox beliefs and avoided the synagogue across the street even on High Holidays. He left home in his early teens, managing to survive as an errand boy for some Lower East Side "businessmen" and supplementing his income by shooting craps in the tenement courtyards and perfecting his skills at the local pool parlor.

It's not clear how he first met my soon-to-be mother, nee Sophie (but at age 13, "Susie, if you please") Dassin, but it must have been Georgie's easy self-confidence that, as she confided to her best friend, Annie, "swept her off her feet." Though not much better off financially than the Goldmans, the Dassin brothers were better educated and more worldly. When they learned that their younger sister was dating Georgie Goldman, her five brothers gave him no credit for his rebellious independence. Seeing him as nothing more than a young punk, they often taunted Susie:

Georgie Porgie, pudding and pie,
Kissed the girls and made them cry,
When the boys came out to play,
Georgie Porgie ran away.

The Dassin family seemed to inhabit a different country from the old-world atmosphere of the Goldmans. Compared to the dimly lit rooms of the Goldmans' railroad flat, where my arthritic grandfather divided his time between davening and listening to the news on his Philco radio, the constant chatter, singing and mandolin playing at the Dassins was like bursting from a dark tunnel into bright sunshine. My mother and her younger sister, Betty, together with their older brothers, were always cracking jokes, hilariously mimicking the idiosyncrasies of relatives and friends, and, best of all, making music. The apartment was often filled with spontaneous performances of Russian and Jewish songs played by the men on mandolins and balalaikas and joined by my mother and Betty, whose lovely voices belied their impending unhappy marriages.

My mother's father, Sam, had been a barber in Odessa before emigrating to New York around the turn of the century. After a shipboard romance and an Ellis Island marriage to an Austrian-born *shayna maidel*, it took a year of odd jobs and night classes in English, before he managed to open a one-chair barbershop on the Lower East side. Barely more than five feet tall, and sporting a bristle of a mustache, he could easily have been a stand-in for the barber played by Charlie Chaplin in *The Great Dictator*. His greatest passion, however, was not the movies, but Italian opera. He was often heard humming the score to "Rigoletto," not to mention "The Barber of Seville," while stropping his razor. Whenever a new opera came to the Met, he would close his shop and rush off to attend the matinee. This behavior not only invited plaintive arias from my grandmother, but eventually discouraged regular customers who did not trouble themselves to consult the schedule at the Met. Eventually forced to sell the business, Sam soon learned that an empty barbershop did not attract potential buyers. His solution was to offer free haircuts to homeless men on the Bowery. That did the trick, and his apparently thriving shop found a ready buyer in an Italian barber who paid the full amount in cash. They closed the deal with a handshake and a hug and Sam insisted on treating his successor to drinks at a local tavern.

"So now you go out at night, too?" my grandmother, Bertha,

said, catching a whiff of the brandy on Sam's breath. She was noticeably taller than her husband, with a full figure and a naturally regal posture that she used to good effect when she stood over him.

"No," he replied, somewhat coyly.

"Oh, you say nothing and you expect me to warm up your supper for you?"

"What's to say?" he said, depositing the roll of cash on the table.

Bertha scooped the money into her apron pocket. "You're robbing banks now?" she said. Sam shrugged.

Georgie Porgie did not run away and, still in their teens, he and Susie married at City Hall. Juggling his various jobs— "keeping my balls in play" was the way he put it—enabled them to afford a cold water flat and pay for the hospital where I was born a few months later. Despite the cigarette dangling from his lips, when my father appeared at the hospital wearing a pair of corduroy knickers the nurses turned him away.

"Boys aren't allowed on the maternity ward," they said. "Besides, don't you know there's no smoking here?"

Starting as a sign of his tough masculinity, Georgie was already smoking more than a pack of unfiltered Camels a day. One of my most vivid childhood memories was crying in my crib in the middle of the night when he would bring me a glass of water. The powerful smell of nicotine on his yellow-stained fingers created an aversion to smoking that stayed with me for the rest of my life.

It was the depth of the Depression and Georgie struggled to support his young family. Jobs were scarce, so he turned to hustling pool and, to my mother's dismay, even boosting merchandise of uncertain origin. But, after my younger brother Ronnie was born, the strain proved too much, and my father was forced to accept his parents' offer to take me in until he "got back on his feet."

I was given the bedroom my father had once shared with his older brother, Archie, who was also "out of the house" having married my mother's best friend, Annie, the year before. The room was now used as a storage area for cast-off furniture and clothing: piles of tables and chairs, broken lamps, even some empty pickling barrels from the delicatessen. What little light there was came from a dusty window that was partially blocked by a doorless wardrobe filled with the camphorous smell of old suits and dresses on wire hangers. There was barely room for my single bed.

I soon developed a ritual before allowing myself to fall asleep. Peeping out from under my blanket, I first made sure that the human shapes in the wardrobe had not come to life and were not about to approach my bed. Then I listened to the muffled voices of the adults in the other rooms, just in case my parents had come to take me back with them. After that, I got into my flying position. I had discovered that, by lying flat on my back with my arms and legs as straight as possible, I would often dream I was flying high above the city. I could feel the wind in my face as I rose above the rooftops, higher and higher into the clouds, with the streetlights twinkling far below. Sometimes, I would soar so high I became frightened I would continue flying forever. But I always managed to find the secret door through which I could return to my bed.

What struck you first when you entered my grandfather's delicatessen were the sawdust-strewn plank floors and the tantalizing smorgasbord of smells: smoked fish; gleaming filets of lox and sturgeon; cured meats; salamis hanging from hooks; aged cheeses; barrels of pickles and sauerkraut; all kinds of nuts and imported olives; and— what mattered most to a child of five—cakes and candies of every shape and color: Turkish delights, halva, licorice, sugared fruit slices, imported chocolates. The aroma of the sweets produced an irresistible counterpoint to the pungent spices that pervaded the air. It was the last surviving store of several my grandfather had owned before the Depression, and it was only through the efforts of my three aunts, who worked long hours behind the counters, that he had managed to keep it open.

By the time I came to live with them, my arthritic grandfather had retired to a corner chair next to the Formica kitchen table where he still did the business accounts in a large ledger he kept on a shelf next to the Old Testament he studied every day. Leaning heavily on his cane, he managed to hobble about, but most days he got up from his wooden chair only twice a day to daven and—an increasing number of times—to go pish. On Shabbat and the High Holidays, his oldest son, Archie, would come over to help the old man negotiate the stairs and cross the street to the Orthodox synagogue. In the morning he read his newspapers—*The Daily News* and the conservative Yiddish paper *Der Tag*. Then he switched on the tabletop radio that remained tuned to the news until well into the evening. I still remember the voice of Gabriel Heatter's sign-on: "There's good news tonight!" Of course, in 1939, the news was anything but good.

In those days, the neighborhood was ethnically divided block-by-block into Irish, Italian and Jewish enclaves. There were few, if any, Black or Latino families. A couple of months after my seventh birthday, my grandfather had me dress up in new short pants and a jacket so that I could accompany him to Yom Kippur services at the synagogue. After an hour, when I began squirming and yawning, he told me to go stand outside for my grandmother to take me home. While I was waiting by myself, a group of Irish boys came by and started taunting me: "Sheeny in a shiny suit! Little Ikey!" they called out. One of them grabbed me by my jacket and we fell to the ground. Just then, my grandmother appeared and the boys ran off. I was not seriously hurt, just a skinned knee and a torn sleeve. That evening, when my grandfather heard what had happened, he took me by the ear and gave me several whacks with his cane. "I'll teach you to fight on Yom Kippur," he said.

I was not aware at the time that my little Yom Kippur scuffle was only a minor part of the periodic rumbles in the courtyards where Jewish, Italian and Irish boys fought with fists and dangerous zip guns fashioned from the right-angled corners of wooden produce crates and topped with heavy rubber bands that worked like slingshots to hurl projectiles of linoleum or even nails. Bleeding casualties from these fights were sometimes carried to my grandfather's delicatessen with pleas to use his phone for an ambulance. He must have had this in mind when, a few days after punishing me for fighting, he handed me a net bag filled with chocolates wrapped in gold foil of the kind he usually gave me for Chanukah. "If you have any more trouble with those boys," he instructed me, "just give them some of these and they won't bother you." Years later, I realized that those candies were tokens of his payoffs to the Bronx mob for "protection."

After school, I often played with Shayna, the youngest daughter of a neighborhood tailor and his *shaytl*-wearing wife who had gained a kind of local notoriety for having given birth to five girls. A couple of years older than me, I admired Shayna's rope-skipping and hopscotch skills. Most of the time, we played on the sidewalk or the front stoop. But one afternoon, I invited her up to my grandparents' apartment for a snack of milk and cookies. Aside from my grandfather who was dozing by the kitchen table, no one else was home when we took our milk and a handful of some of my grandmother's chocolate rugelach into my bedroom. After we gulped down the goodies and were about to go back downstairs, Shayna suddenly took me by the hand and pulled me into the bathroom, locking the door. "Let's play doctor," she said, sitting down on the wooden toilet seat and lifting her dress. "You can examine me." I wasn't sure what she meant. "I don't have a steadyscope," I said.

Just then, my grandfather started pounding on the door with his cane. *"Efenen di tir!"* he shouted. "Open the door!" Both of us frightened, Shayna jumped up and we unlocked the door. My grandfather reached in and pulled me by the hair. "Pfui," he said. "You should be ashamed."

Fortunately, my grandmother had just returned from shopping. She hurried over, a look of concern on her deeply lined face. She took Shayna's trembling hand. "I'll bring her home," she told my grandfather. After that, Shayna and I were not allowed to play together.

I never told anyone about something else that happened while I was living with my grandparents. One afternoon, I was late coming home from school, having stopped at the corner candy store where I tried the owner's patience by reading the latest Superman comic book off the rack. Hurrying back to the apartment, I thought I heard a voice in the downstairs hall. "Uncle Archie?" I called out, thinking my father's older brother had come looking for me. When there was no answer, I peered into the dimly lit stairwell and discovered a tall man in an overcoat and a cap pulled down over his eyes. "Come here, sonny," he said in a low voice. I took a step back. "I won't hurt you," he said. "I just want to show you something." Terrified by his half-smile and hooded eyes, I turned and bolted up the stairs, afraid he would come after me. He did not and I never saw him again. But his shadowy figure troubled my sleep for a long time.

What really gave me nightmares, however, was the first movie I ever saw: "Dr. Jekyll and Mr. Hyde," starring Spencer Tracy and Ingrid Bergman. I had just turned seven when my father's younger brother, Uncle Davy, decided an appropriate birthday present would be for him to take me to see the new version of the film. I still remember the horror I felt when the respectable doctor injected himself with a serum that transformed him into a raging monster. If good and evil could inhabit the same person, how was it possible to trust anyone? Uncle Davy laughed when I gripped his arm as tightly as I could in an effort to hold on to the reality of my world.

That year my grandfather decided I was old enough to sit at the Passover table. It was the one time of year when—with the exception of my parents—the entire Goldman family, including nephews, nieces and cousins, sat down together around the polished mahogany table in my grandparents' dining room with its chinoiserie wallpaper and oval-framed, hand-tinted photographs of relatives from the old country no one ever spoke about. It had taken my grandmother countless trips up and down the three flights of stairs to do the shopping for the ceremonial meal. After my grandfather's blessing of the ritual matzo and nibbling of the *karpas* and *charoset* from the seder plate called for in the Maxwell House Haggadah, the feast began with my grandmother's feathery light matzo balls floating in golden chicken broth, followed by gefilte fish, handcrafted from several kinds of fish she brought home still quivering from the market and kept alive in the bathtub awaiting their destiny. That was only the first course to whet the appetite for the platters of beef brisket, roast chicken and vegetable kugel that followed in quick succession. Possibly the only thing lacking would have been the copious amounts of alcohol consumed by the *goyem* at their feasts.

But my grandfather's droning Hebrew recitation preceding the meal—joined with decreasing enthusiasm by the assembled company—seemed interminable to me. By the time the adults had repeatedly dipped their fingers in the sweet wine and demonstrated their courage by swallowing bits of Manischewitz matzos topped with tiny spoonfuls of my grandmother's fiery horseradish, I began to nod off. I don't know how long I was asleep when I was revived by the clatter of dishes and lively expressions of appreciation directed at my beaming grandmother who continued to circulate the table making sure that no one's plate remained empty for even a moment. Suppressing my dislike of its pale consistency, I took a nibble of the small portion of gefilte fish one of my aunts offered me from her fork. That was when Uncle Davy saved my life.

Unlike my father, Davy had graduated from high school with top grades. His ambition was to become a doctor, but due to the de facto quota system against Jews at the time, his applications to pre-med programs at schools like Cornell and Columbia were repeatedly rejected. Davy never gave up. He continued to send out a blizzard of applications and, in the meantime, practiced using his tongue depressors and stethoscope on me. For some reason, he also thought that hypnosis should be included in his resume. His room was just down the hall from mine, and he would often come in after I was in bed to shine a flashlight and move a pencil back and forth in front of my eyes, instructing me to relax, even though I was already half asleep. I was never sure what he was trying to achieve, but it all came to an end after the US entered the war, and he enlisted as an orderly in the Army Medical Corps. That Passover he was on leave before his departure for an overseas location. So it was my good fortune that he was at the table when I began to choke on a small bone in the gefilte fish that had eluded my grandmother's radar. As I gasped for breath, there was a general tumult:

"Drink some water!"

"Swallow some matzo!"

Uncle Davy fought his way through the crowd of my well-meaning executioners, some of whom were poking their fingers down my throat while others slapped me on the back. Davy picked me up and deftly performed what we now call the Heimlich maneuver. The fishbone popped out onto the table to cries of *"Gott sei dank!"* Then, like a Torah procession, a group of men in yarmulkes and prayer shawls triumphantly carried me off to bed.

Dai-dai-yenu
Dai-dai-yenu
Dai-dai-yenu
Dayenu dayenu!

I never got a chance to thank Uncle Davy, who was killed the following year in North Africa. At a time when European Jews were being forced to brand themselves with yellow stars, my grandfather displayed the gold star for Uncle Davy just above GOLDMAN'S in the window of his delicatessen.

Not long after my encounter with the fishbone, my father's street connections paid off when he was offered a job as a waiter at the Friars Club in Manhattan. My mother said he looked smashing in his uniform with its starched white shirt, white linen trousers with matching suspenders, black three-button jacket and a purple cummerbund encircling his waist.

I'm not sure how he did it, maybe by passing along a few successful betting tips, but he managed to persuade a couple of club members to teach him the rudiments of tap dancing and a few soft-shoe routines, enough for him to take into the tenements on weekends where he tried to talk recent immigrants into giving their children lessons (fifty cents an hour) as a step up the ladder of success.

"It'll give'm a leg up," he told the dubious parents. "Who knows? They could become movie stars."

My father's oldest sister, Tressa, was the one who first made me aware of the pleasures of reading. Most of the books in the apartment were in Hebrew or Yiddish, but Tressa managed to rescue a book called *Russian Folktales* from Uncle Archie's collection when he moved out to live with Annie. I was fascinated by the witch Baba Yaga who lived in a house built on chicken feet, a kind of pre-modern mobile home. Then there was the puzzling random nature of the unfortunate traveler burdened for life by the malevolent Woe Bogiter who had tumbled from a tree onto his shoulders.

It was a great disappointment, not only for me, but for the entire family, when Tressa ran off to marry Sandor, a Hungarian delivery man she had come to know while she worked at the delicatessen. He was a sturdily built, middle-aged man with closely cropped hair and chronically bloodshot blue eyes that looked out defiantly on the world. But when my grandfather found out that Tressa's husband was Catholic, he angrily disowned his daughter and required the family to "sit shiva" for a week, as though mourning her death.

At first, none of this mattered to independent-minded Tressa until it turned out that Sandor's alcoholism led to fits of uncontrollable rage. After a few years of "getting slapped around" as she told my father, she fled with her two young daughters, Josie and Molly, to a small town in upstate New York where she managed to find a job at a Greek diner. With the exception of my father, she avoided the family and became somewhat of a recluse, living with her daughters in a rundown house full of cats. Whenever my father had a good day at gambling, he would send some of his winnings to Teresa, an act of generosity I first learned of in one of her letters after Georgie died.

After Uncle Archie married my mother's best friend, Annie, he found work in a downtown haberdashery. What Archie liked about the job were its regular hours and its location a few blocks from the 4th Avenue bookstores where he browsed almost every evening after work. When he came home, he would greet Annie with a peck on the cheek and sit down to the supper she had prepared, barely responding to her attempts at conversation beyond a few mouthfuls of praise for her cooking. Then he retired to his favorite armchair with a plate of crackers and Gorgonzola or Stilton cheese, poured himself a glass of sherry, filled his pipe from a tin of Prince Albert tobacco, and read until he dozed off. Mostly, he read biographies of military or political figures and historians like Metternich and Burke who confirmed his conservative outlook. Whenever he and my father got together, they would end up in bitter arguments that distressed my sweet-tempered Aunt Annie, who secretly sided with Georgie's liberal (what Archie called communist) views.

On one such visit to Archie's apartment, I noticed a book about airplanes among the hundreds of books in the overflowing bookcase and stacked on the floor. Thinking he wouldn't miss it, I slipped it under my shirt and took it home. A couple of days later, Uncle Archie came by my grandparents' apartment and asked if I had forgotten to tell him I had "borrowed" the book. Sheepishly, I returned it. He thanked me and left.

About a week later, a package arrived addressed to me from Uncle Archie. It was the first time I had received anything but a birthday card in the mail. Wrapped in string and brown paper, was a copy of Booth Tarkington's *Penrod* with a note saying, "Thought you might enjoy this—Archie." For some years after, whether we lived only a few blocks from each other, or across the country, Uncle Archie never failed to send me a book for my birthday and even for Chanukah.

Archie's innocuous appearance, his slumped shoulders and flat-footed walk, served him in good stead in his Sunday occupation as a bookie for the Jewish mafia in the Bronx. Residents of the neighborhood confidently placed their bets with him, trusting that the money would be there in the unlikely— "but you never know"—event of a winner. Although individual bets could be as little as a dime, neighbors would sometimes pool their wagers in the hope of a large payoff that would be shared among the bettors. And one day, lightning struck. The tenants of our building won the lottery. Shouting and laughing, men and women rushed out into the street, forming a conga line that snaked around the block with cries of "We hit! We hit!" And, though he was only a lowly bookie for the mob who had repeatedly taken their hard-earned money, everyone now looked on Uncle Archie as a hero.

Unfortunately, Archie was low-hanging fruit for the captain of the local police station, anxious to meet his monthly arrest quota without ruffling too many feathers. Archie was tried for illegal betting and sentenced to thirty days in the 46th Precinct jail.

"Those shysters in City Hall call that a crime?" the haberdashery owner exclaimed, promising to save Archie's job for when he "got back from vacation."

None of this would have bothered Archie too much—the captain even looked the other way when Archie arrived at the jail with some books and his pipe and tobacco—had it not been for the shock he received the day he was released: Aunt Annie had taken advantage of his absence by selling his entire book collection to a used book dealer, not averse to taking advantage of her ignorance.

Yet Archie and Annie never divorced. Suppressing his feelings of anger and betrayal, Archie went about methodically rebuilding his library. And a year later, Annie gave birth to twin daughters.

Chapter 2

On the morning of December 7, 1941, I was finishing my soft-boiled egg in my Donald Duck egg cup, when an urgent announcement interrupted the program on my grandfather's kitchen radio: Hundreds of Japanese warplanes had attacked the U.S. naval base at Pearl Harbor, sinking many ships and killing more than two thousand Americans. The next day, President Roosevelt declared war on Japan, and a few days later, we entered the war in Europe against Nazi Germany.

"*Gott sei dank,*" said my grandfather.

Several of my uncles were soon drafted, but Archie was classified 4F due to his flat feet. My father's draft number was sufficiently high for him to escape induction. And due to the growing manpower shortage, he was able to find a job as a sales rep for a sewing machine company in Bridgeport, Connecticut. While the salary was not high, he would have the use of a company car and earn a commission on the sales he made. My mother was thrilled. They finally had the resources for our small family to get back together. Sight unseen, they rented a house in Easton, Connecticut, an easy commute from my father's job.

The country was at war; the Nazis were on the march, herding European Jews into concentration camps; and we were boarding a

Greyhound bus headed toward the happiest year of my childhood.

The bus stop in Easton was at a two-pump gas station that offered "anti-knock" leaded gasoline. We went inside the adjoining general store to ask for directions to the house we had rented. Even though my aunts had taken me a few times to S. Klein's department store in Union Square, I had never seen a store like this one. In the center of the room, surrounded by a few chairs, was a working wood stove next to a stack of split firewood. Crates of root vegetables, beans, and potatoes filled the room with an earthy smell, utterly different from my grandfather's delicatessen. Rows of sturdy leather boots stood next to woolen hats and gloves, denim pants and jackets, plaid flannel shirts, overalls and winter coats. Another section displayed canvas tents, skis and snowshoes just like the pictures in a Thornton Burgess book Archie had sent me. There were tools of every kind, some even my father had never seen before.

"My boys want to know what you call that twisty tool there," he said to one of the clerks.

"I guess you're not from around here, the clerk replied. "That's an auger for ice fishing."

"Why do you fish for ice?" my brother Ronnie asked.

"Good question," laughed the clerk.

The rifles and shotguns that lined one wall reminded me of the Western movie Uncle Davy once took me to see. "They must still fight Indians here," I whispered to Ronnie.

"That's enough," my mother said, shooing us toward a table offering donuts and cider with a sign saying "USO-Support Our Troops." Carrying both heavy suitcases, my father caught up and asked the woman behind the table for directions. A tall man, wearing suspenders and a red and black woolen shirt, put down his glass of cider.

"Maybe I can help you," he said. I know the place you're looking for. It's about a mile from here."

"Is there a taxi we can take?" my father asked.

"Nope, but it's no trouble for me to drive you in my delivery truck if you don't mind sitting in the back." He put out his hand. "I'm Steve Willcox," he said.

"George Goldman," my father replied.

"Goldman, eh?"

"Is that a problem?"

"Not for me," Willcox replied. "Though there may be a few around here who listen to Father Coughlin on the radio."

"We call him Father Coffin," my father said.

"That's pretty good," Wilcox nodded.

"Who's Father Coughdrop?" Ronnie piped up.

Everyone laughed and Willcox picked up one of the suitcases. When he dropped us off, Willcox refused to take any money. Instead, he wrote down his telephone number and said, "I'm pretty handy at fixing things. Let me know if you need any help."

At first, none of us could believe that the two-story colonial house, with a mailbox out front labelled Top O'Knoll, was to be the home of a Jewish family just off the bus from the Bronx.

"Is it an Irish house?" I asked.

"No, it's not like O'Reilly," my father laughed. "Top O'Knoll means top of the hill."

Though the house was relatively modest, it might well have been a mansion in the eyes of my mother. Not one to appear overly impressed, my father couldn't help a "hump, hump" nod of approval when we entered a room with a fireplace and floor-to-ceiling bookcases. "It's called the study," he informed us.

We trooped up the wooden staircase to the three dormer ceilinged bedrooms on the second floor. After a brief inspection, my parents deposited their suitcases on the double bed in the room with two windows, described as the "master bedroom" in the real estate listing. Ronnie and I decided to share a somewhat smaller room with twin beds. My mother said that the third room at the end of the hall could serve as our guest room. As it turned out, we never had any overnight guests, so Ronnie and I came to call it "the ghost room."

Without bothering to unpack, Ronnie and I raced downstairs to explore the backyard.

I took aim with my imaginary rifle when we spotted a brown rabbit nibbling on some wilted leaves in what remained of the kitchen garden. We raced up the hill to a large shed whose creaking door reminded me of the "Inner Sanctum Mystery" program I used to listen to on the radio with Uncle Davy. For a moment, I hesitated to enter the gloomy room, but Ronnie grabbed my hand and pulled me inside where the walls were lined with dozens of tools like the ones we had just seen at the general store.

Suddenly, Ronnie gasped. "What's that?" he exclaimed, pointing to a mounted deer head on the back wall, its glass eyes staring down at us as though the animal were still alive.

"It's a deer head," I said.

"Yuck. Why'd they tack it to the wall?"

"To show off that they shot it."

"I don't like show-offs," Ronnie said.

The day after we arrived, my father was down in the basement trying to figure out the coal-fired furnace. "I know from poker, not stoker," he grumbled, loud enough for us to hear. Ronnie and I were with my mother in the kitchen when the doorbell rang. Surprised, the three of us went to the door where we found two matronly women dressed in pleated skirts, high-buttoned jackets and neatly perched narrow-brimmed hats. One of them was holding a plate of chocolate chip cookies.

"Good morning, my name is Linda Wetherbee and this is Doris Carlsen," the taller one chirped. "We heard that your family has just moved to town, and we'd like to invite you to attend Sunday services at our church."

My mother looked confused.

"It's the Methodist Church at the crossroads," Linda explained.

"But I'm afraid we're Jewish," my mother said.

Doris took a step backwards and one of the cookies fell to the ground. Ronnie scooped it up and popped it in his mouth.

"Well...that's all right... you're still welcome... and welcome to town," Linda stammered.

"Yes, and welcome to the cookies," Doris said, thrusting the plate at my mother. A little unsteady on their high heels, our visitors retreated down the grassy knoll.

The cookies were delicious. And as it happened, the cub scout troop I later joined met in the basement of the Methodist Church. I learned all kinds of useful skills, like how to tie a hitch knot, what to do if you got bitten by a timber rattlesnake, and how to whittle the wooden spigots used to tap the sugar maples in the spring. But my mother was furious when I told her that the scoutmaster, Mr. Junger, insisted on calling me Jacob, not Jack or Jackie, because—he told me with a wink—"I'm on to your people's tricks." At our next meeting, my mother marched into the church basement and asked Mr. Junger to step outside. After that, my name at roll call was Jack.

At Halloween, my parents allowed me to go trick-or-treating with some of the kids after school. I decided to go dressed as a magician, with a pencilled moustache, old top hat, and a magic wand. In those days, people gave out apples and homemade cookies and invited us in to admire our costumes.

At one house, with a grinning jack-o-lantern on the porch, the elderly retired teacher made a great show of trying to guess who we were in our costumes before handing us our treats. When my turn came, he hesitated a moment and I heard him mutter—more to himself than to me— "terrible things happening...terrible." Then he took an extra handful of candy and put it in my bag.

True to his word, Steve Willcox stopped by occasionally to check out how we were doing. One snowy Sunday he came to the door and told my father "George, we really appreciate your efforts to keep the neighborhood warm, but you might want to close your windows when you turn on the furnace."

That year, my parents had no objection when I joined the school chorus and learned to sing Christmas carols. It wasn't long before we two kids and my mother started singing "Jingle Bells" and even "Silent Night" at home. On the day school let out for the holidays, my nice third grade teacher, Mrs. Phillips, asked if anyone's family was without a Christmas tree. I was the only one to raise my hand. That afternoon, she drove me home with the class tree in the trunk of her car.

When my mother answered the door, she stared at the fully decorated tree, trailing silver tinsel on the welcome mat.

"Jackie told us you didn't have a Christmas tree, so we'd like you to have the class tree," Mrs. Phillips explained. It took a moment for my mother's innate politeness to prevail: "That's very thought... ful of you," she stammered.

That evening, when my father got home from work, he stared at the tree leaning against the coat rack in the hallway.

"Where did that come from?" he asked, surprised.

"I had to accept it," my mother explained.

"Then let's set it up in the living room where it belongs," my father said with a mischievous grin.

My brother and I were delighted. And it was all my mother could do to restrain Georgie from taking a photo of us by the tree to send back to his father in the Bronx. We didn't exchange presents or anything like that. On New Year's Day, my father dragged the tree outside and chopped it up for firewood. Ronnie managed to rescue a few of the paper angels.

I spent much of my time during Christmas vacation reading in the study at Top O' Knoll. It was there that I discovered writers like Mark Twain and Charles Dickens. There was also a floor-standing Victrola next to a shelf of classical vinyl records. At first, my favorites were "The Carnival of the Animals" and "Peter and the Wolf", but I gradually started listening to Beethoven symphonies, some Bach cello suites, even a few Mozart operas that I played over and over.

One evening in late spring of our second year at Top O'Knoll, my father did not return home from his job in Bridgeport. My mother tried not to appear worried when my brother and I went to bed. It was well past midnight when the telephone woke us.

"Georgie! Where are you?" my mother exclaimed. "Grand Central Station?" she said, disbelievingly. "What are you doing in Grand Central Station?"

She began to cry when my father confessed that, for some time, he had been hustling pool in Bridgeport, recklessly pocketing his winnings without giving the local mobsters their cut. When they found out, they came after him, and he had to run. About to board the 20th Century Limited for Los Angeles, he promised to send for us as soon as he "was situated."  And with the wartime economy booming, it didn't take him long to find a job driving a forklift truck at the Port Hueneme Naval Station, about fifty miles west of Los Angeles.

Chapter 3

Over our tearful objections, my mother helped us pack what we could into a few suitcases. She arranged with Mrs. Phillips to store the rest of our belongings at the school until we could send for them. Trying her best to paint it as an adventure, like the wagon trains heading west, my mother corralled Ronnie and me onto the bus to Grand Central Station. The train was crowded with young soldiers and sailors in uniform on their way to the war in the Pacific. Perched on a top bunk we shared in the Pullman section, Ronnie and I tried to identify the ranks and insignias of the servicemen parading the narrow aisles. Our attractive mother, with her hair combed in the then-popular victory rolls style, ignored the wolf whistles directed her way, perhaps in the premonition that many of those boys would not live to outgrow their adolescent fantasies.

My mother's older brother, Julie, was waiting for us on the platform when we arrived at Union Station in Los Angeles. His clear blue eyes, high forehead, and aquiline nose combined with a disarming smile gave him an appearance of sympathetic intelligence, a family trait he used to good advantage in his burgeoning career as a Hollywood director.

"Look at you, Jackie," he exclaimed, rumpling my hair. "You're almost as tall as me!" Then he swooped up my brother Ronnie with one arm and drew my mother to him with the other. They kept kissing and hugging until Ronnie grew impatient and wriggled to the ground.

My mother let out a gasp of astonishment when Uncle Jules led us to his cream-colored Buick convertible. Ronnie and I clambered onto the plush leather seat in the back and, with the top down and the music of Tommy Dorsey on the radio, we drove along palm tree lined Figueroa Boulevard. A gentle breeze brushed my hair, and a memory came to me of my adolescent parents dancing in the kitchen when I was a baby:

Heaven, I'm in heaven,
And the cares that hang around me through the week
Seem to vanish like a gambler's lucky streak...

Over lunch of hamburgers and vanilla malts at the Pig 'n Whistle restaurant on Hollywood Boulevard, Uncle Jules assured my mother that we could stay with them for as long as it took to find an apartment we could afford. "Georgie has a good job now and you can start looking when he gets here over the weekend. There's nothing for you to worry about," he said, giving her cheek a pinch. Left unsaid was his Hollywood success that enabled him to help out his "kid sister." The luxurious Buick convertible parked outside said it all.

It was only a short ride to Uncle Jules' house on Bronson Avenue where he dropped us off. "Bea and the kids are expecting you," he assured us. "I have a meeting with Charles Laughton about my next film, but I'll see you tonight."

Aunt Bea and our three cousins were waiting for us at the door. Before her marriage, Bea had a promising career as a classical violinist. After graduating from The Juilliard School of Music while still in her teens, she soon became the second chair violinist with the New York Philharmonic Orchestra and often played with chamber music groups on the radio. Now, in her late 30's, she seemed not to regret having abandoned her career for the role of mother of three children and the wife of a talented and ambitious film director. Aunt Bea's sacrifice may also have been compensated—at least in part—by the employment of Lois, a full-time maid, whose service enabled Bea to practice her instrument and perform with string quartets at the homes of movie stars and Hollywood executives.

After our initial greetings, Aunt Bea and my mother continued their conversation, leaving us children to awkwardly size up one another. Cousin Joe, a year older than me and the beneficiary of a private school education and music lessons, was the first to break the silence by inviting me and Ronnie to accompany him up to the attic where he had something to show us. Joe's younger sisters, Ricky and Julie (yes, Julie) seemed relieved to be more or less dismissed.

When we arrived at the attic, Joe switched on the light to reveal an elaborate model train layout. Set in a landscape that included urban streets and buildings and rural farms and meadows with miniature cows and grazing sheep, the tracks filled the entire room. Joe started up the freight train with a steam engine that emitted real smoke followed by some fully loaded box cars. It came to a stop at a crossing with warning lights and bells, allowing a sleek passenger train to speed by. Ronnie's eyes popped and I was speechless.

On Saturday afternoon, my father arrived from Port Hueneme in the used Model T Ford he had just bought from a fellow worker. ("No used car lot middleman," he later informed my mother.) Uncle Jules gave him a slap on the shoulder on his way out the door. "Good to see you, Georgie," he said. "Got a tech rehearsal for my next film. Hope to see you tonight."

"I'm afraid we can't stay," my father replied. "I saw an ad in the paper this morning for a house for sale in the Valley. They're asking $4,000 and, now that I have a good job, I thought I could swing it with a loan. But we need to get out there right away, before somebody else snaps it up."

"Have you got a down payment, Georgie?"

My father hesitated. "A hundred and fifty."

"That won't be enough," Jules declared. "Wait here a second."

When he returned, Jules handed my father a roll of bills. "It's a thousand bucks," he said. "Don't worry about paying me back."

My father said nothing about the "loan" from Jules as we hurriedly packed our suitcases and bundled into the Model T. Lois rushed out with a bag of avocado and cream cheese sandwiches. "Can't have your sons goin' hungry," she said, passing the bag through the window to my mother. Georgie saluted her as he drove off.

After a few wrong turns and directions from a couple of gas station attendants, we pulled up at a small house at the intersection of two dirt roads off Van Nuys Boulevard in the San Fernando Valley. It was a modest Cape Cod style bungalow featured at the time as a kit in Sears Roebuck catalogs. There was a small front lawn shaded by several tall walnut trees. In the back, a one-car garage with a badly damaged roof looked like it was about to collapse.

"It's cute," my mother said.

Just then, we saw a middle-aged man, dressed in a suit and tie, shaking hands with a young couple on the front doorstep.

"For Christ sakes," my father exclaimed, as he jumped out of the car. "We may be too late!" We followed him as he hurried up the flagstone path to greet the agent who was still waving goodbye to the young couple.

"Is the house sold?" he asked, without bothering to introduce himself.

"Almost," the agent replied, with a doubtful glance at us.

"What do you mean, almost?"

"Well, the nice couple you saw just leaving made a satisfactory offer I'm about to accept."

"How much?" Georgie demanded.

"Well—if you must know—three thousand eight hundred dollars," the agent said, stressing every syllable.

"We'll take it for four thousand. And here's a thousand down in cash," my father said, producing the roll of bills Uncle Jules had given him.

My mother looked at him in astonishment.

"Now here we are settled in our home in California—If one may call it settled with so many countless things to be done," my mother wrote in a June 1944 letter to Aunt Annie back in New York. She related the "freak lucky streak" that enabled her and Georgie to come up with the down payment on the house in the San Fernando Valley.

"The house and grounds had been badly neglected and that was the reason we got such a wonderful buy. We paid $1,000 down and we are paying off the balance at the low rate of $35 per month." She goes on to describe "the adorable little house which is Cape Cod in architecture and features a living room with a large window facing west. Right here you may fill in the most beautiful skyline of blue-purple mountains, casting an unbelievable pink mist into the blue face of the heavens. Can you picture it?"

Chapter 4

Left unmentioned in my mother's letter, was the discovery my brother and I made when we opened the closet in our bedroom: On the floor was a pile of Stetson cowboy hats, leather-fringed vests, inlaid boots, chaps, spurs, belts with silver buckles and two—unfortunately empty—holsters. Hi-yo Silver! Away!

Only later did we learn that the previous owner of the house was a movie actor named Buck Jones, famous for his cowboy roles in over a hundred Westerns. A few months before we moved in, Buck Jones had lost his life among the many fatalities in the tragic Cocoanut Grove nightclub fire in Boston. That cast a sobering light on the "freak lucky stroke" that had enabled my parents to buy the house on such favorable terms.

At the risk of appearing ridiculous, I dressed myself in some of the adult-size gear to parade before my new friend, Norm Sargent, who lived down the road from us on a small ranch. I had already begun to tag along with him after school when he did his chores "out back" feeding the horses, milking the goats and cleaning the barn.

"What in the heck are you supposed to be?" Norm laughed as I approached.

"A cowboy."

"Ain't no such thing as a Jew cowboy."

Norm's father, who was nearby fixing the barn door, came over and slapped his ear.

"Don't you pay him no mind," he said to me. "He's just jealous of your fancy duds."

Norm and I remained friends. One of our favorite games was to dig foxholes in one of the vacant lots. At a given signal we would emerge from our hiding place to mow down the invading Nazi soldiers. Of course, we knew all the military songs—"From the Halls of Montezuma to the Shores of Tripoli" ... "Anchors Aweigh My Boys" ... "Off We Go Into The Wild Blue Yonder"—that we sometimes sang as we attacked. But we always celebrated our inevitable victory with our favorite song: Spike Jones' "Der Führer's Face":

Wenn der führer says we is de master race
We heil (fart) heil (fart) right in der führer's face
Not to love der führer is a great disgrace
So we heil (fart) heil(fart) right in der führer's face...

Another new friend was a girl named Bonnie Nürnberger who lived on a chicken farm across the road from us. She was three years older than me, with long blonde hair and blue eyes. Soon after we moved in, she had come over with her mother, Mala, to welcome us to the neighborhood. They gave us a dozen fresh eggs and Mala told us what a nice job we were doing fixing up the house. She spoke with an accent that reminded me of my grandparents' Yiddish, but my mother said it was different: It was German.

Bonnie's house was even larger than Norm Sargent's. There was a wide front lawn fronted by a rail fence lined with large cactus plants. Behind a scrim of eucalyptus trees, the back acre had hundreds of wire cages for laying hens. Most wondrous of all, when Ronnie and I first laid eyes on it, was the swimming pool bordered with Mexican tiles and a diving board at the deep end. Bonnie told us we were welcome to come over for a swim any time we wanted. We took advantage of her offer, making sure no one else was around as we bobbed on tiptoe toward the deep end, only to splash back to safety after a few gulps of the chlorinated water.

If Bonnie happened to join us, Ronnie and I hoisted ourselves onto the ledge at the shallow end to watch. Dressed in a two-piece bathing suit that already inspired my admiration, she would take two quick steps onto the diving board and plunge into the water with barely a splash. Later, when I went to see the Esther Williams movie, *Bathing Beauty*, at a Saturday matinee, I couldn't help thinking of Bonnie.

One Saturday afternoon, when Bonnie and I were playing hide and seek at the Nürnbergers' house, I ran to hide in her parents' bedroom closet. In the darkness, I failed to notice anything at first. But when I stumbled over a pair of leather boots, I tried to recover my balance by catching hold of a jacket on one of the hangars and found myself clutching a Nazi uniform, just like the ones I had seen at the movies. Horrified, I ran home.

"He's a Nazi spy!" I shouted to my father, who was raking the front lawn.

"Who is?"

"Bonnie's father, Fritz. I just saw his uniform!"

"He's not a spy," my father laughed. "He's a movie actor. You must have seen one of his costumes."

After that, I got used to seeing Fritz preparing for a shoot in one of his uniforms. Over six feet tall, with a powerful frame and chiseled features, when dressed in a gray-green jacket, gold-braided cap and knee-high leather boots, he looked the very model of a Waffen-SS officer. He rarely got a speaking part, but I remember one exception when he had a scene with a fellow Wehrmacht officer preparing to depart for the front. For days, Fritz strode through the house rehearsing the single word he had to say:

"Cigarette?" he intoned, gesturing with his hand.

Then a barking "Zigarette!," uncertain whether it sounded better in German.

Sometimes, Fritz paid me a quarter just to do my homework near the kitchen telephone while he worked with the chickens. What he hoped for was a call from one of the movie studios for another bit part.

Another source of after-school income at the Nürnbergers was candling eggs for a penny a piece. Mala explained that the tiny blood spots that sometimes appeared in the yolks were harmless, but people didn't like them for "aesthetic" reasons. I thought it might have something to do with my grandfather's religious scruples.

Bonnie did not have time for these after-school odd jobs because she had to practice the accordion. Day after day I heard her dutifully squeezing out poorly rendered attempts at songs like "Lady of Spain", punctuated by little puffs from her lips to blow the wisps of blonde hair from her eyes:

Lady of Spain, I adore you
Right from the night I first saw you…

I was ten years old, and Bonnie was my first crush.

Unlike the sturdy brick building of my school in Connecticut, the Sherman Oaks Elementary School, where I entered the 5th grade that fall, consisted of about a dozen one-room clapboard cabins on a dirt lot surrounded by a chain link fence.

The dusty playground featured a baseball diamond, mostly used for kickball; a couple of tetherball poles; a few sets of caroms and checkers on wooden stands; and several redwood picnic tables with benches, shaded by some towering poplar and eucalyptus trees.

Soon after the semester began, the chain link fence was divided into sections for each classroom where the scrap paper we collected in our neighborhoods was stacked for the wartime paper drive. At the end of each month, prizes were awarded to the class with the highest pile. Once, my class won and we were rewarded with a trip to Universal Pictures where they were filming a Tarzan movie starring Johnny Weissmuller and Maureen O'Sullivan. We giggled when we saw Tarzan swing on a rope over a lagoon no larger than a swimming pool. But Cheetah, the chimpanzee, both charmed and scared us with his nimble acrobatics and sad, intelligent eyes.

In school we learned that Washington chopped down a cherry tree when he was a boy, but did not lie; Lincoln was shot by an actor who was mad at him for emancipating the slaves; and Father Junipero Serra walked the entire length of California, teaching the Indians how to build Catholic missions so they could worship God properly. My parents were proud of me when I brought home report cards with almost all A's.

But Mala Nürnberger urged my parents to round out my education by enrolling me in a ballroom dancing program at the Studio City school where Bonnie was in an advanced class. My objections, and even my father's raised eyebrows, did little to dissuade my mother who bought me my first new suit and a pair of black leather shoes at Ohrbach's Department Store, where I got to ride the escalator.

When I entered the large hall for my first lesson, the dancing master, Dimitri Botinck, a slender figure in tight-fitting black trousers and a billowy white shirt, greeted me with a slight bow. Placing his hand on my waist, he led me across the room to a girl he introduced as Patricia, my dancing partner. To my dismay, Patricia was clearly older and almost a head taller than me. Botinck put on a record of Strauss waltzes and began gliding around the hall with an invisible partner, demonstrating the proper form. And even though Patricia did not hesitate to take the lead, it was evident that I had not inherited my father's dancing talent.

The following week, I invented as many excuses as I could to avoid my dancing class—a headache; losing one of my new shoes; too much homework. But nothing seemed to work. After another dismal lesson, I came up with the bright idea of rolling around in the manure behind Norm Sergeant's barn just before Mala was to drive Bonnie and me to Botinck's studio. "Ooh you smell like a pig!" Bonnie exclaimed as I plopped myself in the back seat. Mala ordered me out of the car and drove off without me. My mother gave me a thorough scrubbing that night and punished me by withholding my portion of her home-made lemon meringue pie that Ronnie quickly gobbled up. It was understood that my dancing lessons were over.

But Mala was not easily discouraged from her efforts to round out my education. When she suggested music lessons, my mother remembered how I enjoyed listening to classical music on the Victrola at Top O'Knoll. It had not occurred to me before, but the idea of learning to play an instrument appealed to me. Recalling the rich tones of Pablo Casals playing the Bach cello suites, I said I might like to play the cello. Mala nodded her approval and, a few days later, my mother and I took the bus to the only music store in town, Babcock's Music on Van Nuys Boulevard, down the street from the hardware and feed stores.

"We don't have cellos," the clerk informed us, pointing to the display of drums and brass instruments. It was evident that the store catered to the local school marching bands. Lifting a gleaming alto saxophone from its stand, he put it in my hands.

"Now wouldn't you like to play a beautiful instrument like that, sonny?"

He turned to my mother. "You can rent it for a year and the payments apply to the purchase price. Not only that, we have teachers here and your son can take lessons every week in one of our studios."

"It looks good on you," my mother said.

So that's how I came to take saxophone lessons from Sid Burbank, a soft-spoken musician in his 30s with melancholy grey eyes and the hands of a classical violinist. He told me he sometimes played in after-supper clubs, but mostly he was a studio musician. When he asked me what kind of music I liked, I told him Prokofiev and Beethoven.

"And you want to play the sax?"

"I guess."

"Well, the saxophone started out in France as a classical instrument," Sid mused. "So we can start out that way and see where it leads."

From then on, most of my assignments were simple violin exercises Sid had transposed for the alto sax. As I progressed, he gradually introduced sheet music for marching bands and even a few popular tunes like *White Christmas* and *Sleepy Lagoon*. I enjoyed Sid's gentle patience, and I never questioned his failure to encourage me to improvise or even to listen to jazz. For him, I would remain a nice Jewish boy—bright, but hopelessly square.

My lessons with Sid came to an end after about a year when I began to notice a kind of nervous edginess on his part. Sometimes, in the middle of a lesson, he would mumble "right back" and go out to his car for a few minutes. Finally, one Saturday Sid failed to show up at all. I asked one of the clerks at Babcock's if anything had happened to him. He whispered in a conspiratorial tone that Sid had gone "into rehab." I wasn't sure what that meant, but I was afraid to ask because it reminded me of how my grandparents in the Bronx used to whisper about people who had cancer.

Chapter 5

That year, just before Christmas, I was awakened by a loud argument between my parents. Of course, I had heard them argue many times before, but this was different. My mother's sobs were louder, and it sounded like they were scuffling in the kitchen, making the dishes rattle. Frightened, I left my brother still sleeping as I climbed out the bedroom window and ran across the road to the Nürnbergers.

"Jackie!" Mala exclaimed when she saw me shivering at the door. "What's wrong?"

"My parents are fighting and…" Without letting me finish, Mala took me by the hand to the kitchen where she poured me a glass of milk. Then she telephoned my parents. When my embarrassed father hurried over, Mala and he had a whispered conversation. By that time, Fritz had entered the room and Bonnie stood in the doorway, rubbing her eyes. When Mala offered to have me stay with them until things settled down, Fritz nodded, and Bonnie flashed me a big smile.

"We have plenty of room," Mala said, "and Jackie can help us decorate the Christmas tree." My father couldn't suppress a grin. But by the time he went back to our house, my mother had already called Uncle Jules to come for her and Ronnie. Though Mala may have guessed the whole story, Ronnie and I were never told why our parents were fighting.

I did help the Nürnbergers decorate their freshly cut tree with beautiful hand-blown glass ornaments they had brought with them from Germany. Even Fritz had to use a ladder to place the winged angel on the top branch of the floor-to-ceiling tree. On Christmas day, Bonnie and I munched on chocolate-covered marzipan cookies while we unwrapped our presents. The Nürnbergers gave me a gift that even rivaled the books received from Uncle Archie: a Gilbert chemistry set.

Some might have called it an act of God, but my father's more modest explanation was that a Camel cigarette saved his life. A couple of weeks after the argument that split up our family, he was taking a smoking break near the forklift truck he drove at the naval base. Suddenly, a cable broke on one of the overhead cranes, spilling a shower of heavy lead pipes to the floor below. There were several injuries, and two men were killed, but my father did the dance of his life, barely managing to leap aside just as his truck was crushed. However, one of the pipe fragments struck his head, throwing him to the floor. When my mother got the call from the hospital where he was being treated for a broken left arm and a possible concussion, she rushed to his bedside where, amid tears and kisses, they made up.

Uncle Jules gave me a bright red Schwinn bicycle for my 10th birthday. That summer, exploring the roads further than I had ever walked, gave me a sense of independence that soon took the form of a paper route delivering the *Valley News*. Every day after school I went to the small grocery store on the corner for my bundle of papers that I folded like table napkins and loaded into the saddlebags on the back of my bike. On really hot days, I would down a Dr. Pepper before setting off on my route, tossing the papers into the front yards of subscribers. Once a month, I knocked on doors to collect the subscription fees, from which I deducted my two- dollar- a -week wages. At my mother's urging, I opened a college fund savings account at the local bank.

Among my subscribers, Rhoda and Charlie Morgan lived down the road from us in a converted barn with some caged rabbits under the windows, a couple of tethered goats, and ducks and chickens running free in the front yard. Rhoda did house cleaning and Charlie was a handyman at the Nürnbergers. Charlie had a tight-lipped appearance and didn't like to waste much time talking, but he could fix practically anything. Sometimes, Rhoda would invite me and Ronnie to come over for her home-made pie and ice cream, more than enough incentive for us to listen patiently to her repeated stories of how she and Charlie had made their way from Kansas to California during the Depression and how fortunate they felt having found steady work at the Nürnbergers. Even more special, were the times she welcomed us to spend the night in their double bunk bed. After Ronnie clambered up to the top bunk, Rhoda would tuck us into the eiderdown quilts she had sewn with the soft feathers from their ducks. Falling asleep, I felt like I was floating in clouds. Her "wake up lie-abeds!" roused us at break of dawn to a ranch hand breakfast of eggs, bacon and pancakes. She smiled at us as we gobbled down the food. But I sometimes had the feeling that she was sad because she had no children of her own.

One Saturday afternoon, I bicycled over to the Morgans to collect for their subscription to the *Valley News*. As usual, I leaned my bike against their rail fence and walked across the dirt yard to their house. After downing a glass of goat milk and chatting with Rhoda for a few minutes, I went to retrieve my bike, only to discover that it was gone. I ran to tell Charlie who was outside splitting firewood for their stove. Driving his hatchet hard into one of the wood pieces, he shouted to Rhoda "Some sidewinder swiped Jackie's bike!" Then we jumped into his Ford pickup and raced around the nearby roads. But there was no trace of the thief.

Since I could no longer deliver papers without my bike, I decided to apply for work at one of the nearby tomato farms where I had seen Mexican kids even younger than me bent over the vines. The foreman looked me over doubtfully, but said they were shorthanded, and he'd give me a try. He showed me how to twist the ripe tomatoes off the vine and put them in metal buckets that, when filled, weighed more than 20 pounds each and had to be carried two at a time to the dumpster at the end of the row. "You get ten cents a bucket" the foreman told me. "So you can make a buck an hour, easy. Not bad for a kid. Of course, you get docked for bruises."

Summertime temperatures in the San Fernando Valley often approached 100 degrees. And around two o'clock in the afternoon, my mouth felt dry, and sweat was running into my eyes and ears. One of the field hands noticed my stress: "Por que no sombrero, gringo?" he asked, clucking his tongue. Looking around, I realized I was the only bareheaded one in a sea of caps and straw hats. An hour later, I began to feel dizzy, and I dropped the buckets I was carrying. The last thing I heard was someone shouting "Socorro!"

I woke to a nurse bathing me in ice water. "You had a sunstroke," she said, pressing a wet sponge to my forehead. "But you'll be alright. Lucky they got you to the hospital so fast." When my parents were allowed to visit me that afternoon, my mother sobbed and kissed my forehead. "Guess you almost kicked the bucket," my father said. I was released a couple of days later, but became delirious in my sleep, and when my father came to my bedside with a glass of water, I punched him in the eye. His arm was still in a sling, so he told people that his black eye was also due to the accident at the naval base

Late that summer, Uncle Jules bought me another bicycle for my birthday and my father, who had fully recovered from his injuries, was unexpectedly drafted in the call-up for D-Day. He was ordered to Fort Ord on the coast at Monterey Bay. Despite her severe case of varicose veins, my nine-month pregnant mother insisted on seeing him off at the train station. A few weeks later, we received a picture postcard from Georgie with a scenic view of the bay. "Having a wonderful time," he wrote. "Wish you were here."

With rumors flying about a possible allied invasion of France, we were apprehensive that my father would be sent overseas after finishing his basic training. That didn't happen. Possibly, it had something to do with a high-stakes poker game with some of his officers, but we never found out how Georgie managed to secure an assignment with the Army Special Services entertainment branch. Granted a two-week leave when my sister Laurie Ann was born, he told us "I landed on my feet, not in Normandy."

"Hey kid, where's your faddah?"

I was on my hands and knees weeding the strawberries in our victory garden when I saw the black and white wing-tipped shoes planted next to me. Looming over my head was a giant tree of a man in a dark suit topped with a wide-brimmed fedora hat.

"He's not here," I said, scrambling to my feet.

"When will he be back?" the fleshy lips smiled, revealing a gold-capped tooth.

"I don't know. He's in the army."

"The army? I'll be damned." He shook his head. "I can't see him fighting in a foxhole."

"He's not," I replied. "He's a tap dancer."

"Sonofabitch!" fatface guffawed. "Ya gotta hand it to Georgie. He even figured out how to con the army."

His stubby fingers reached into his pocket and—instead of the gun I expected—he handed me a business card:

Gino Ricci
General Contracting

There was a telephone number, but no address.

"Give this to your faddah the next time you see him," he said. Then he walked back to the black car waiting for him in the road with a driver at the wheel.

"You take care of yourself, kid," he shouted out the window as the car pulled away.

Chapter 6

After my father got out of the army, my mother tried to tether his gambling while he looked for a job. But every once in a while, like a good trainer she gave him some leash. On one of those occasions, to my surprise, she suggested that he take me with him to Las Vegas. Maybe she thought my straight-arrow innocence would be a restraining influence or that the trip could be a bonding experience between my father and me. In any case, we set off in the pre-war Plymouth my father had bought from Norm Sergeant's father, who had an auto repair shop. Like most cars at the time, ours had no air conditioning. So just before entering the scorching Mojave Desert we stopped at a gas station for one of their cardboard boxes with holes in it that the attendant filled with dry ice. He showed us how to secure it in the window on the passenger side and I still remember that cool breeze on my face as we crossed the desert toward the lights of Las Vegas that rose from the landscape like a shimmering mirage.

I was disappointed when we drove past the neon sign of the Flamingo Hotel and checked into a cheap hotel on one of the side streets. "We're here on business," my father said, "not to live it up." I tried to get comfortable on my lumpy mattress next to a window fan that rattled like an old jalopy. I could hear someone coughing through the wall behind my bed. None of this seemed to bother my father, who was already snoring while I lay with my eyes wide open, staring at the cracks in the ceiling.

The next morning, we walked past a row of casinos and pawn shops to a diner where we had a breakfast of steak and eggs. "Meals here are cheap," my father explained. "They like to keep the chumps happy." After breakfast, we walked to the brand-new Golden Nugget Casino where my father handed me a roll of nickels to play the slots while he headed for the poker tables. There was a sign saying you had to be over eighteen to gamble, but no one paid any attention to me.

The thing about my father's gambling was that he knew when to stop while he was ahead. So he was in a good mood the next morning when he told me we would be heading home after breakfast. As I was washing my hands in the casino bathroom, I noticed a colorful dispenser attached to the wall and I asked my father to buy me some candy.

"It's not candy," he said. "Let's go."

"Is it gum?"

"No, I said c'mon."

"What are Trojans, then?" I demanded, reading the label on the dispenser.

"That's enough," he said. He took my hand in a tight grip and led me out to the car. Lured by a sense of forbidden knowledge, I continued to pester him as we drove off.

"Why can't you tell me anything? I bet you don't even know. I'm gonna tell mom."

Finally, he pulled the car over to the side of the road. "Get out," he ordered, leaning over and opening the door. So I got out and he drove off. I'm not sure how long I stood there by the side of the road, but it was long enough for me to be afraid that he was not coming back. Some cars sped by, and then a produce truck stopped.

"Do you need a ride, sonny?" the driver called out. Frightened by his twisted grin and bony knuckles gripping the steering wheel, I took a step back from the road.

"No, my dad's coming right back," I said, preparing to run if he opened the door of his cab.

Just then, my father screeched to a stop on the other side of the road. I dashed to the car, and as we made a U-turn alongside the truck, my father—quick to size up the situation—gave the driver the finger. We drove the whole way back in silence. When my mother ran out of the house to greet us, I was about to blurt out what had happened. But she looked so happy when my father handed her the roll of fifty-dollar bills he had won, that I decided not to say anything. I never did tell her. Over time, it became an oath of Omerta between my father and me, a sort of bond, though not the kind my mother might have hoped for.

After his success in Las Vegas, my father slipped his leash and began gambling again. Whenever he had the chance, he placed his bets at boxing matches at the Olympic Auditorium, horse races at the Santa Anita track, and, from time to time, he even persuaded my mother to go with him to Las Vegas. They would take off on a Friday afternoon, promising to return on Sunday. I was left in charge of my three-year-old sister and my brother, with instructions to call Rhoda Morgan if I needed help. Actually, Rhoda showed up without my having to call her, never failing to bring us a home-cooked supper. Nevertheless, my anxiety increased after my brother and sister went to bed on Sunday. I would sit by the living room window and count the headlights of passing cars on the dark road until my parents' old Plymouth finally pulled up in front of the house.

My father eventually found a well-paid job as a traveling salesman for a glass manufacturer in Paso Robles. But the company was forced to downsize due to lower prices from competitors in Mexico and, after a year, my father was laid off. My mother did her best to help out by working as a script editor for the Hollywood director, Douglas Sirk, a German émigré and friend of the Nürnbergers. But it was not enough to support a family of three children, and one day, my brother and I asked who were all those strangers trooping through our house. My mother began to cry when she told us the house was for sale.

Like a movie played backwards, Uncle Jules drove us to Union

Station, and we headed back East where one of my father's old pals had offered him a job in a jewelry store. We rented a courtyard apartment in Rego Park, a neighborhood in Queens. I entered 9th grade at Jamaica High, at the time, one of the best-rated schools in the New York system. Unaccustomed to such a large urban school, with its undercurrent tensions between black and white students, I felt like I had parachuted in from another country and I made few friends. Instead, I started taking sax lessons with a musician named Sy Green, who played in pit orchestras on Broadway. He not only played alto sax, but could double on almost every reed instrument, as well as the flute. He was amused when I told him that I mostly played transposed violin exercises with my previous teacher, so he assigned me some Broadway tunes. But when I asked about jazz, he simply smiled and shook his head. "I don't think that's your cup of tea," he said. Years later, when I began going to jazz clubs, I understood what he had meant.

I also took a weekend job going door-to-door in Rego Park selling synthetic sponges, a new product from Dupont. My father joked that I was helping those Dupont robber barons sponge off everybody. "Still, it's better than picking tomatoes," he said, reminding me of my earlier attempt at financial independence that had cost him over a hundred dollars. Just as Ronnie and I were beginning to find new friends at school, my father revealed that Long Island hadn't panned out the way he had hoped. So, at the end of the semester, my patient mother once again packed our belongings and we boarded the train back to California, where my mother's youngest brother, Eddie, had agreed to give Georgie a job in the packing department of his imported cashmere sweater business.

While we were still living in Rego Park, my mother's parents had joined their children in Los Angeles, where Uncle Jules helped them buy a two-bedroom house in Van Nuys. Sam found work as a barber at the Veterans Hospital and Bertha busied herself with the fruit trees and grapevines in their backyard that reminded her of the Austrian village she had lived in as a girl. They rented out the spare bedroom to Howie Nebenzahl, a young orderly at the hospital who frequently entertained giggling nurses in his room.

At the back of my grandparents' yard, was a small building that may once have served as a tool shed but had been cleaned and painted to serve as a guest house, albeit without running water. That's where I was installed after our return from Long Island, with the rest of our family moving about among relatives until we could afford to live together again.

That fall, I decided to try out for the football team at Van Nuys High. I was skinnier and faster than many of my classmates, so I made the team as a second-string left halfback. But, as luck would have it, our starting player in that position, Bob Waterfield, had already attracted the attention of college scouts with his broken-field prowess. So my action was confined to those brief moments when Waterfield ran to the sidelines to catch his breath. But, in the final quarter of the last game of the season, I finally got my chance. We were playing against Eagle Rock High, a team of farm boys notable for their beefy linemen, one of whom managed to tackle Waterfield with such force that he was momentarily stunned and had to come out of the game.

"Goldman!" the coach shouted. "Get in there."

Grabbing my helmet, I ran onto the field, and though everyone in the stands was still on their feet out of concern for Waterfield, I felt like the hundreds of eyes were on me alone. On third down, the quarterback handed me the ball and I raced down the field... Not very far. The same bruiser who had tackled Waterfield threw me to the ground and one of his teammates, unable to stop his momentum, inadvertently punched a hole in my knee with one of his cleats. Timeout was called and I was helped to the sideline where the team doctor examined my knee. "It's just a shallow puncture," he said. Then he poured some iodine into the wound and bandaged it. By that time, Waterfield had run back onto the field and our bouncing cheerleaders were leading the stands in the school chant:

Ala vevo, Ala vivo, Ala vevo, vivo vum,
Bum getta rattrap bigger than a cat trap,
Bum getta rat trap bigger than a cat trap,
Cannibals, Cannibals, sis, boom, bah,
Van Nuys High School, rah, rah, rah

In the locker room, after the game, which we had won thanks to a twenty-yard touchdown run by Waterfield, the coach tried to console me.

"Don't worry, Goldman," he said, "you're sure to make the team next season."

"Nope," I replied. "I'm going to join the marching band."

"Why would you do that?"

"At least I'd get more time on the field."

Coach laughed and slapped me on the head.

If I had to describe the difference between my grandmothers, I'd say that Grandma Goldman was the kind of woman who would wipe a child's snotty nose, while Grandma Dassin would hand the child a handkerchief. To put it another way, I never had to get to know Lena Goldman, I just knew her. But it was only after I began writing letters for her, that I came to know Bertha. Unable to write in English (though she spoke several languages), she took the opportunity to enlist my help. The signal was a glass of milk and a plate of homemade cookies waiting for me on the kitchen table after school. Most of the letters were to her sister, Ida, in New Jersey and they all began the same way: "Dear Ida, you should only know," followed by a list of Sam's most recent crimes. Sometimes, for emphasis, she would throw in expressions like "Believe you me," or "God only knows." As a fifteen-year-old with limited experience, I had no way of knowing what was true and what was Bertha's surmise. It reminded me of the opera records I used to listen to at Top O'Knoll. Though she knew little about opera, Bertha saw Sam as a Don Juan and she had cast herself as the affronted Donna Elvira. You might say that I was the librettist.

As it turned out, my residence in my grandparents' backyard was short-lived. Less than a year after I moved in, Grandma Bertha caught pneumonia and died.

An elderly rabbi intoned a few prayers in Hebrew at the funeral parlor where my mother and the rest of the Dassins sat on wooden chairs in the front row, receiving whispered condolences from the Hollywood colleagues of Uncle Jules and Aunt Julia's mahjong friends. I sat with my father and Ronnie in the second row, where I did my best to restrain him from kicking the chair in front of him out of boredom. The limousine in which we rode to the cemetery, with its black upholstery and white silk ceiling, looked to me like a mobile version of the open coffin in which Bertha's body had been displayed. It was the first time I had worn a yarmulke since my faux bar mitzvah.

A few months after Bertha's funeral, Sam had a fatal heart attack—So, who is to say? As Bertha might have said.

Chapter 7

Not long after Sam's funeral, my father "hit it off" in Las Vegas with a wealthy Chinese businessman named Walter Lee. By coincidence, Lee was in the same business as Uncle Eddie: importing cashmere sweaters from Taiwan sweatshops. Sensing an opportunity, Georgie touted his "considerable experience in the *schmatta* business," not bothering to mention that he had been nothing more than a lowly packer for my Uncle Eddie. Not bothering to check his story, Lee offered Georgie a position with a company he was starting in San Francisco.

"The Sky's the Limit", my father sang, imitating Fred Astaire's tap dance as he told my mother about his latest job offer.

With our departure imminent, my mother suggested that I could move from the guest house in the backyard into my grandparents' bedroom.

"I think I'll just stay where I am until we leave," I said.

"But wouldn't you be more comfortable in the main house? Howie is almost never there and I'm sure he wouldn't care."

"It's not Howie that bothers me about sleeping in Grandma's room."

My mother gave me a hug.

Once the semester ended, we boarded a coach car on the Southern Pacific's Streamliner train to San Francisco. Ronnie and I took turns pressing our noses to the window as the California landscape whizzed by. After we arrived, we spent a few magical days at a downtown hotel "on Walter Lee's tab," my father boasted. Ronnie and I were thrilled when my parents succeeded in renting a three-bedroom row house in the Sunset District, only a block from the ocean. I drew the long straw with Ronnie for the bed by the window that I opened on our first night just enough to hear the sound of the waves that lulled me to sleep. In the morning, my father drove off in his company car to the downtown building where he had his own office— the first time in his life.

A few weeks after we had settled in and Ronnie and I were enrolled in our schools, my mother was thrilled when Walter Lee and his wife invited my parents for dinner at an upscale French restaurant.

"Dad's boss, Walter, is such a gentleman," my mother told Ronnie and me at breakfast the next morning. "He held my chair when we sat down and spoke French with the waiters. Dad and I couldn't make head or tail over the menu, but Walter said not to worry. First, we were served cups of delicious consommé, then came a parade of small plates, with bits of fish, poultry, beef and vegetables, so nicely arranged that it seemed like a shame to eat them. At first, I didn't know which fork or knife to use, so I tried to copy Walter's elegant wife, Emoretta, who had been a fashion model before their marriage. For dessert, Walter ordered the French trifle, which was anything but. It came with a thimble of black coffee that you couldn't pick up without extending your little finger, like some pretentious snob in the movies. As if all that wasn't' enough, we were then served what they called 'digestifs', a French word I could understand. When we got home, I told your dad how proud I was of him and…"

As she was about to continue, Ronnie interrupted: "Mom" he said, "I think we're gonna be late for the school bus."

My tenth-grade English teacher at Lincoln High School, Danielle Lamoreaux, had curly auburn hair and emerald cat eyes. She was the prettiest teacher I had ever seen. I made sure to sit in the front row, but when she recognized my eager hand in answer to a question, I sometimes forgot what I was about to say. After a while, the girls in class began giggling and giving me funny looks, so I moved to the back of the room. I wasn't sure if Miss Lamoreaux noticed.

I did alright in my other classes, but it was the track team that kept me from daydreaming over Danielle. After I made the cut as a sprinter, our coach, Marco Ferrucci, decided that I would compete in the 100- and 220-yard dashes. Our star sprinter was a kid from Jamaica named Ace Marley. Thinking of my year in Jamaica, New York, I told him we may have gone to the same high school. "I like your attitude, mon," he laughed, "but I think you have the wrong latitude." During the course of the semester, I became accustomed to the sight of Ace's muscular calves striding ahead of me. But Coach Ferrucci's rigorous after-school regimen helped me to develop into a reliable third-place runner in our intramural track meets. Toward the end of the year, I had collected enough bronze medals for Ferrucci to start calling me "Bronzino."

That year, our team did well enough to qualify for the All City track meet in San Francisco's Kezar Stadium. I made myself my pre-meet breakfast of two lamb chops and a glass of orange juice and tried to ignore the butterflies in my stomach as we boarded the bus to the stadium. I was especially nervous because my father had promised to be in the stands along with one of his poker buddies, Jim Murphy, a strapping red-headed Irishman who was a supervisor at the Department of Public Works.

After a brief pep talk from Coach Ferrucci, we did our warmup exercises and waited for the events to begin. Unlike Marley, who had qualified for both sprints, I was only running the 100-yard dash in the finals. When I headed for the starting blocks, Jim Murphy let out a whoop I tried to ignore as my father waved his program at me. Fortunately, I lived up to my nickname and took third place. But while I was catching my breath, Coach Ferrucci ran up to me.

"Bronzino," he said, "stay loose, you're going to have to run the 440."

"But Coach, I've never run the 440," I protested.

"Well, now's your chance," he said.

It turned out that our 440 specialist had pulled a hamstring while warming up and couldn't compete. As for Marley, he was still out of breath after having won first place in both sprints. To make matters worse, the 440 featured a Hawaiian kid named Kaholo from Mission High School who had already broken the city record.

"Just try to stay on Koholo's heels," Ferrucci told me.

In those days, the 440-yard dash was run once around the standard quarter-mile track. But in Kezar Stadium, the first 100 yards started under the stands in what was called the tunnel, not visible to the spectators. I lined up in the blocks along with Koholo and the other runners. The gun went off, and sprinting out of the tunnel, I was ahead of the pack by a good ten yards. My father and Murphy sprang to their feet shouting their encouragement. Coming around the first turn, I could hear someone closing in on me, so I ran as hard as I could. Then Koholo passed me on my right, and I could see his smooth, almost effortless stride. I tried to stay on his heels, but it was no use. At around 300 yards, it felt as though someone had kicked my legs out from under me. Then the entire pack pounded past me, and I came in last.

"Bronzino," said Coach Ferrucci, shaking his head, "did you forget which race you were running?" In the locker room, Murphy patted me on the head. "That's alright, Jackie boy," he said, "you really showed them for the first hundred yards."

On a Saturday morning just after school let out for summer vacation, my father woke my brother and me while it was still dark outside. "Get dressed," he said, "we're going fishing with Jim Murphy."

Coming from my father, the invitation was so unusual that I thought I was dreaming. But when I heard Ronnie exclaim "Oh boy!" and saw him give our grinning father a hug, I put aside my doubts. We gulped down some corn flakes and milk, packed a few peanut butter sandwiches and drove off to meet Murphy at a boat rental on San Francisco Bay.

"Have you got a landlubbers' special today?" Murphy asked the attendant.

We rented the largest rowboat with two sets of oars, along with four fishing poles and life preservers.

"We're expecting a king tide today, so be sure to get back here before one o'clock," the attendant instructed.

"Yah, yah, ye sound just like me sainted mother," Murphy interrupted, in his best Irish brogue.

We set out with Murphy and my father rowing briskly until we were about a mile from the shore. Then they pulled up their oars and allowed the boat to drift with the tide back toward shore. My father tuned the portable radio he had brought along to some dance music. It was a beautiful morning with blue skies and a gentle salty breeze. Murphy showed Ronnie and me how to bait our hooks with bits of anchovy and we threw our lines into the water. For close to an hour, we had nothing more than a few nibbles on our lines. Suddenly, Ronnie's pole began to bob and dip with some force.

"Hold on there, lad!" Murphy shouted. "Feed him some more line!"

After a few minutes, with my father's help, Ronnie pulled in a three-pound shad. The fish flopped and slithered around the floor of the boat until Murphy managed to remove it from the hook and dump it in a bucket of water.

"Well done, boyo," Murphy said. Ronnie beamed with pride.

We dropped anchor and continued fishing for another hour or so, but none of us had any luck. Then my father glanced at his watch: it was already a quarter to one.

"I guess we'd better head back," he said, remembering the attendant's admonition.

"If you say so, Georgie," Murphy reluctantly agreed.

"Anchors aweigh, me boys!" Murphy sang out, and he and my father began to row. After a while, I noticed that an onshore wharf seemed no closer than when they began rowing.

"I don't think we're moving," I said.

"Pish, pish," Murphy said. "Keep rowing, Georgie. We're doing just fine."

They continued pulling on the oars, but when they stopped to rest, it was clear that the boat was drifting steadily out into the bay.

"What's that big rock we're heading to?" I asked.

Murphy turned his head. "Well boys," he said, "I fear we're going to Alcatraz."

"The prison?" my father asked.

Just then, we heard the roar of an engine as a speedboat rushed toward us.

"Don't move! Put your hands on your heads!" said a loud voice on a megaphone.

"Just do as they say," Murphy whispered, as the patrol boat pulled up to inspect us.

"What are you doing here?" the amplified voice asked.

"Ah, don't worry lads!" Murphy shouted. "We're not planning a prison break. Just a hapless crew drifting with the tide."

The patrolmen looked us over. Then they laughed. It took them an hour to tow us back to shore.

"I warned you to get back before one," the dock attendant growled.

"So you did," Murphy replied. "We should have listened to your bad tidings. Anyway, the boat's in one piece and we're okay, even though there might be easier ways to catch a fish." He hoisted the bucket with Ronnie's fish, but the attendant was unimpressed.

That night my mother broiled the shad with onions and herbs and Murphy proposed a toast: "To our successful shad-row," he said, lifting his glass.

Not long after our adventure in the bay, my father came home

55

from work with the news that Walter Lee had decided to transfer him back to L.A. to take charge of a new branch of his business. "Just as we were settling in here," my mother sighed. Georgie took her in his arms. "I know," he said, "but I couldn't turn it down. It is a kind of promotion, and the salary is even better."

    I went down to the rocky shore and wrote a farewell letter to Danielle Lamoreaux. Then I tore it up and threw the pieces into the waves.

Chapter 8

We rented a modest house in North Hollywood with the expectation that, once my father had proved himself in his new position, my mother's dream of a house in the hills overlooking the ocean would come true. But it was not to be. The "office" my father was supposed to manage turned out to be a small room with a desk and chair whose sole function was to receive packages from Taiwan and Hong Kong that he was to deliver, unopened, to addresses that would be telephoned to him every morning. Georgie quickly understood that importing sweaters was only a cover for Walter Lee, whose real business was smuggling drugs. To his credit, the same day he was given these instructions, my father walked away, not even bothering to lock the door behind him.

"I can't believe it," my mother said when Georgie told her why he quit. "Walter seemed like such a gentleman." But she did not shed a tear when Lee was eventually sent to prison.

Unlike his previous setbacks, my father did not bounce back from having been "played for a sucker" by Walter Lee. He became depressed, sitting in the kitchen all day, chain smoking cigarettes. My mother did her best to cheer him up, but when he turned down her offer to go with him to Las Vegas, she knew he needed help.

Unlikely as it may seem, it was my father's older brother, Archie, who managed to help—or perhaps shame—him out of his despondent mood. Archie, Annie and the twins had joined the family trek to the West Coast, and he had landed his dream job as manager of a men's clothing store on Brooklyn Avenue in the Boyle Heights neighborhood of East Los Angeles. He didn't beat around the bush when he drew up a chair next to my father.

"Feeling sorry for yourself, Georgie?" he said. "Well, I don't know what happened to you and I really don't want to know. But it's time you stopped acting like a spoiled kid. We've all had our ups and downs. How do you think I felt when Annie sold all my books while I was in jail? But I didn't sit around mooning about it. And whatever it is you did—or someone did to you—it's time to get over it. You have a family to support, so *sei ein Mann*."

Somehow, Archie's blunt treatment of his younger brother worked. The next morning when we went into the kitchen for breakfast, my father was gone. My mother couldn't conceal her worry when we didn't hear from him for several days. Finally, he called from San Luis Obispo to say that he had found a good job as a traveling salesman for a furniture manufacturer. My mother told Aunt Annie to thank Archie for helping Georgie get back on his feet. "Now we'll be able to pay the rent and put food on the table again," she said. "And guess what? Georgie is getting a new bed for Laurie Ann— wholesale!"

Soon after we had moved to North Hollywood, I noticed the boy next door shooting baskets through a hoop attached to his garage. That was my introduction to the Richards family, where I came to spend most of my afternoons, not only playing basketball with Freddie, but in conversation with his parents, Olga and Gene. Olga was a professor of sociology at UCLA, and on some mornings she gave me a ride over the Cahuenga Pass to Hollywood High where I had enrolled for my senior year. Gene was a self-taught tool and die maker for a plastics manufacturer. As a young man, he had worked in a General Motors auto plant in Flint, Michigan where he took part in the storied 1936 sit-down strike that led to the recognition of the United Auto Workers Union. Now, when he returned from work in the late afternoon, he would pour himself a glass of beer and sit down at the spinet piano he had built from a kit. Usually, he played the music of Charles Ives and Samuel Barber, composers I had never heard of.

At first, the Richards and I talked about movies and the novels I liked—I had just begun reading *For Whom The Bell Tolls*. One morning on the way to school, Olga asked me what I thought about the war in Korea. I said I didn't know much about it, but I was sure we would defeat the Chinese—after all, we had the atom bomb. The truth was, that while my parents were liberal Democrats who strongly supported FDR and the New Deal, we had no doubts that, when it came to war, we were the good guys. I assumed that was also Olga's view, but she changed the subject.

That Saturday, after shooting hoops with Freddie, Olga invited me in for a cold drink. Gene was tinkering with something that he put aside when I came in.

"I wanted to ask you something about Hiroshima," he said.

"You mean the atom bomb?"

"Exactly. Have you ever read about what happened when we dropped the bomb?"

"Sure, the Japanese surrendered."

"No, I mean what happened to the city."

I thought for a moment. "Well, I guess a lot of people died."

"You mean a lot of civilians—including women and children."

He went over to a bookcase and pulled out a copy of John Hersey's *Hiroshima*.

"You might want to read this," he said, handing it to me.

Chapter 9

My closest friends at Hollywood High were Peter Gottlieb and John Gruen. Some students called us the three G's, others, less kindly, the three nerds. In a way, that was unfair to me because, while Peter was a math whiz, and John could reel off by heart long passages from Shakespeare, I was what you might call a plain-vanilla good student. Peter had the look of an alert beagle, perpetually tensed to spring. By contrast, John shambled along in his food-stained shirts and wrinkled trousers, totally unconcerned about his appearance. On weekends, we sometimes hiked in the hills near the Griffith Park Observatory where we pondered Nietzsche's influence on Dostoevsky and why chamber music was on a spiritually higher level than symphonies. Once John asked us if we knew that Hegel's concept of the consciousness of consciousness was basically the same as the story of Adam and Eve's expulsion from Paradise. "They lost their innocence, that is to say, their unmediated existence in the world, when they ate from the tree of knowledge." Peter, who was more scientifically inclined, asked if he had learned that in Sunday School.

Occasionally, we continued our discussions at John's Hollywood apartment that he shared with his divorced father, John Sr., a prune-faced screenwriter whose drinking habit had finally drowned what talent he may have had. He called us "The Three Vestal Virgins," and when he learned that Jules Dassin was my uncle, he sneered: "That Commie. Be sure to wipe that shit off your shoes before you come in here."

On a hot September afternoon, I was waiting for the bus on Hollywood Boulevard when I heard someone call my name. It was Billy Draper, a trombone player who was a year ahead of me at Van Nuys High. We slapped fives and I asked him what he was doing after he graduated.

"I'm majoring in music at USC," he said. "But guess what? I started my own dance band. We've been playing proms, parties, bar mitzvahs—you name it. We call ourselves The Curtain Calls. Get it? Billy Draper and The Curtain Calls."

We exchanged phone numbers and, a couple of weeks later, I got a call from Billy, inviting me to join his band.

"Our third alto ran off with some floozie and we're booked for a Mickey Rooney wedding party next month. It's a big deal for us and I could really use you."

I thought about it for a moment, then I told him I was used to being third. So why not? When I told my mother, she insisted on taking me to Bullock's Department Store where she bought me the maroon jacket with brass buttons and blue suede shoes that Billy's band wore. She told me I looked smashing.

Mickey Rooney's wedding party at a Beverly Hills hotel was for friends who had been unable to attend the ceremony in Las Vegas to an actress named Elaine Devry. It was the first wedding for Billy's band, though the same could not be said for the groom. After our second set, we took a fifteen-minute break, and I went to the bar for a Coke.

"Don't you go to Hollywood High?" a tall blond girl approached me.

"That's right," I said. "I'm a senior."

"I thought I recognized you. My name is Sue Levine. I'm here with my father, Mel, who's a friend of Mickey's."

She told me she was also a senior and planned to go to Reed College in Oregon after she graduated.

"It's too bad you're playing tonight, and we can't dance."

I told her I wasn't much of a dancer anyway, but maybe we could have lunch together sometime.

"I'd like that," she said.

It wasn't long before Sue invited me home with her. The Levines lived in a two-story Spanish style house with a balcony and a tiled roof in the Hollywood Hills, not far from the iconic Hollywood sign, fastened like a nametag on the bosom of an overeager hostess. Sue's mother, Estelle, a former actress with flowing cornsilk hair, appeared in the winding streets every morning with a pair of best-in-show Afghan hounds. I gradually grew accustomed to seeing the hairy back of her father, Mel, bent bare chested over his typewriter. He had written numerous B movies with titles like "Bandit of Sherwood Forest" and "Robin Hood of El Dorado". While none of his films were blockbusters, his steady output provided the family with what Estelle called a "comfortable living", but to me, seemed like fabulous wealth. Needless to say, there was a faint whiff of amused noblesse oblige in her parents' manner toward their daughter's boyfriend who, lacking transportation, often walked the four miles from his house in the Valley to their home in the commanding heights.

Though Sue's high cheekbones and popsicle-pink lips qualified as attractive—even by high school standards—she made no effort to join the sorority of thoroughbred beauties with their pleated skirts and angora sweaters. Tall, with a sinuous build and alert hazel eyes, she had twice led the girls' tennis team to city championships. I often thought I would have had much more competition for her favors had not her air of independence and sharp wit intimidated most of the boys. Though I felt flattered, I puzzled over Sue's interest in me. She was the self-confident daughter of worldly parents with social status, while my restless father had us living like nomads, pitching our tents from coast to coast. And though I insisted on paying whenever we went to a movie, it was Sue who picked up the tab at the Hollywood restaurants she favored. She may have suspected that, before we began dating, my idea of fine dining was a rack of barbecued spareribs and potato salad at the counter of the Pig Pig diner on Van Nuys Boulevard.

Even more difficult for me to navigate were the hootenannies at the actor Will Geer's house in Topanga Canyon. Sue had been attending these for several years and she naturally assumed that I would accompany her. But, unlike most in the dungaree and gingham-clad crowd, I was unfamiliar with the lyrics of the international roster of folk songs. I did my best to join in a few songs like "This Land is Your Land" and "Hallelujah I'm a Bum". But when Pete Seeger struck up the resonant chords of "Viva La Quinta Brigada", the best I could do was to silently mouth the lyrics like a goldfish navigating its glass bowl.

If my social awkwardness bothered Sue, she didn't show it. Though I was dimly aware that I myself was the offspring of pre-marital sex, it never occurred to me that the strict boundaries of our petting in Sue's bedroom was an indication that, for her, our relationship was nothing more than a high school infatuation. I was still naive enough to believe that the "real thing" would have to wait until our wedding day. Meanwhile, I tried my best to pull my shirt down over my damp-stained pants and avoid her parents as I slunk off home.

It was a blue-sky afternoon in May, and I was sitting on the high school lawn at lunchtime with Peter and John when my father pulled up in his car and honked the horn. I ran over and he handed me an opened envelope with the return address of the California Institute of Technology. "Go ahead, read it," he urged. The letter said they were pleased to inform me that I had been accepted to the freshman class at Caltech. Except for the time he won the trifecta at the Santa Anita racetrack, I couldn't remember such an expression of happiness on my father's face. He stuck out his hand through the window and pumped my arm up and down. "Put 'er there pardner," he said. Then he drove off. Of course, for my fellow nerds this was nothing exceptional. They had already accepted similar offers from MIT and Princeton. Re-reading the notice from Caltech, I was too embarrassed to ask what "full stipend" meant.

Chapter 10

Since I had no other school expenses, my father proudly stepped up to pay for an off-campus room I intended to share with one of my Hollywood High classmates, Eugene Epstein. "That's Ep-Stine," he was always correcting people. "You don't say Steenway piano, do you?" His father owned the Pickwick Bookstore on Hollywood Boulevard, one of the first in the country to offer a large selection of paperback books and a favorite after-school hangout for the nerds. For some reason, Eugene was not part of our clique at Hollywood High, possibly because he had no interest in our lofty philosophical discussions, and he struck us as having to slave too hard to achieve top grades. Once, he invited me to his home, not far from the Levines in the Hollywood Hills, where he showed me a 1930s Bally pinball machine he had restored to working order.

We drove out to Pasadena in Eugene's new two-door Packard, a graduation gift from his parents. Eugene told me he intended to major in astronomy and that he had brought along a new 3.5-inch Questar telescope that he planned to install in our bedroom window. I told him I had not yet decided on a major, but I was thinking of chemistry because I had heard from Peter Gottlieb that Linus Pauling was one of the best professors at Caltech. I didn't mention my fond memories of the Gilbert chemistry set the Nürnbergers once gave me for Christmas.

In addition to Chemistry, the freshman curriculum at Caltech included Plane and Analytical Geometry, Physics, and Basic Graphics. For the first few weeks of the semester, I followed Eugene's example, dutifully addressing my homework before tumbling into bed late at night. Gottlieb was right about Pauling whose lively presentation and wide interests attracted visitors from all over, even to his freshman lectures. I was less fortunate in my physics class, where the rapid-fire approach of a brilliant young instructor seemed to assume abilities that I lacked, despite the slide rule that we all wore on our belts like medieval daggers. I was bored by the endless plotting of graphs in Analytical Geometry and, as for Basic Graphics, it was hopeless. Even in high school, I had failed Mechanical Drawing due to my difficulty visualizing three-dimensional objects. But at least my high school teacher, Mr. Mcdonald, was entertaining. He would unpack his lunch and thermos bottle of coffee while the class attempted to draw some object he had placed on a stand. Occasionally, he interrupted us by smacking his lips and saying "mmm macaroons." Then he would stick out his set of false teeth, clamped on the sticky confection.

It was not long before I realized that, at Caltech, I was far from being among the most gifted students who—at least in my insecure imagination—seemed to spend their time playing chess and cards in the lounges while effortlessly sailing through their exams. To make matters worse, halfway through the semester I received a letter from Sue:

Dear Jack,

I apologize for not writing sooner, but I needed time to sort out my thoughts and feelings. What it comes down to, is I think we need to take a step back and see what the future brings. I've talked this over with my father and he says it's a sign of growth, only to be expected at our age. He also wishes you the best. I know you'll be disappointed, but I won't be coming home for the Christmas holidays. Someone I've met here has invited me to his family's place in Vail, Colorado where I'm going to take skiing lessons (wish me luck). I'm sure you'll agree that it's best to be honest about these things, and I want you to know that you'll always have a special place in my heart. Also, I'm confident you'll succeed in whatever path you choose. I don't expect you to reply to this letter, but I hope we'll find a way to remain friends, whatever may happen.

Love,
Sue

I was devastated. Sue had been the girl of my dreams. But, at the same time, I had to admit to myself that I had long dreaded the day I would wake up and she'd be gone. I fell into a depression and found it increasingly difficult to concentrate on my courses. A few nights later, I had a disturbing dream:

I am walking along the bank of the creek near our little house in Van Nuys. It is a sunny day and there is a warm breeze. I can hear the buzzing of honeybees hovering over the alfalfa blossoms in a nearby field. The creek is usually dry, like the Arroyo Seco, but now it is filled with the runoff from an unusually heavy thunderstorm. Every now and then, I toss a leaf or a small twig into the rippling water and watch its twisting course downstream. After a while, the breeze seems to have died and it is getting hot. I feel drops of sweat on my face and neck. Thinking to cool off, I kneel down and bend over the water that has somehow grown still. My father's face looks up at me from below the surface. His arms and legs are limp, and bubbles rise from his lips as he silently mouths the words: "Help me...Help me..." I reach down to pull him out of the water, but as I get closer, I realize that he is not pleading for help at all. He is saying "I'm free.... I'm free..." I draw back and watch him slowly sink to the bottom.

When I awoke my arms and legs were rigid and covered in sweat. Even after I showered, I felt like I was sleepwalking, unable to shake off the dream. I decided to skip Pauling's class and walk the several miles to the Japanese Garden near the Huntington Library. I had only been there once before, but I remembered it as a peaceful spot. It being a weekday morning, there were only a few visitors when I arrived. I found a bamboo bench overlooking the koi pond. The only sound was the occasional splash of a fish and the rustle of lilacs and gingko trees near the arc of the Moon Bridge. After a while I caught a glimpse of my own reflection in the water, and I tried to imagine what it must feel like to drown.

A couple of weeks later, when I went to lunch at Dabney House, one of the student houses where I had meal privileges, I was struck by the subdued atmosphere. Instead of the usual clamor that occasionally culminated in boisterous food fights, most of the tables were unoccupied and students were gathered in small groups engaged in hushed discussions. I soon learned that, for the second time, a freshman from our class of one hundred eighty had committed suicide.

No doubt that is what the counselor had in mind when I later went to see him about my depression. After listening to my halting attempts to describe my confusion, he promptly urged me to take a leave of absence from Caltech. "I'll recommend that you receive incompletes in your courses," he told me. You still have your full scholarship, and you can return next fall once you've sorted things out." I couldn't decide whether his worried look was more out of concern for me or for the school.

Eugene offered to give me a ride back to L.A.

"It's too bad," he said. "Next week there's going to be a full occultation of Jupiter I wanted to show you through my telescope."

My mother greeted me with the gentle resignation to which she had gradually schooled herself. My father's response was different. It was only then that I realized the full extent of his pride at my having been accepted to Caltech. "Taking a break?" he said, bitterly. "Give me a break. You're throwing away your life. You're never going back there." Something told me he was right.

Chapter 11

A few weeks later, I was shooting hoops with Freddie when Olga beckoned me inside. "I've been thinking about everything you told us," she said. "You mentioned that you've been reading a lot and thinking about doing some writing. What about transferring to UCLA next semester, where you could take classes in literature and creative writing. Tuition is only a few hundred dollars and you're living at home, so it's affordable—besides, I can drive you to campus."

"Well, I guess you're not a complete dropout," my father said, when he agreed to pay the $40-dollar incidental fee at UCLA. "At least they don't hold you up for tuition," he noted with satisfaction. Because I had only incompletes to show for my time at Caltech, I had to transfer as a freshman. But with courses in English, Psychology, Journalism, and World Literature, far from feeling like a failure, I felt liberated.

Nevertheless, it bothered me that my returning home posed an additional financial burden on my parents, so I signed up for a work-study program that led to a part time job in the laboratory of an Israeli professor, Dr. Itzhak Perelman. On my first day, he explained that his research involved radioactive iodine uptake in the thyroid glands of rabbits. He didn't bother to explain how this might relate to human physiology. In any case, that was not my affair. My humble responsibilities involved washing the glassware, feeding the rabbits and cleaning their cages. In those days, there was a rather casual attitude toward exposure to radioactivity. So I was not particularly concerned that the Iodine-131 Dr. Perelman injected into the rabbits was stored in ordinary flasks with no particular safety precautions.

But, toward the end of my first week on the job, something occurred that may have saved my life. I was sponging down one of the cages when Dr. Perelman sliced open the belly of a rabbit in order to remove its kidneys. Until that moment I was not aware that—ostensibly to avoid chemical contamination—he did not anesthetize the animals before the surgery. My heart skipped a beat when I heard the poor creature's high-pitched scream. I took off my apron and ran out of the lab. I don't know if Dr. Perelman even noticed my absence, but the next day I told him I was quitting. He didn't seem particularly bothered. I was able to find another job mowing the campus lawns and, a few years later, I learned that Dr. Perelman had died of cancer, possibly due to radioactive poisoning.

At the beginning of my sophomore year at UCLA, I joined the staff of the student newspaper, *The Daily Bruin*. As a cub reporter I was kept busy with routine assignments—social events, faculty promotions, new construction on campus. "Who even reads this stuff?" I asked the editor, Bernie Segal. A couple of weeks later, he called me into his office.

"Goldman," he said, "I thought about what you asked me, so I'd like you to take on a feature story."

Flattered, I waited for him to continue.

"I want you to interview Colonel Wiley T. Moore, the commander of the campus ROTC."

"You've got to be kidding," I said. "You know how I feel about ROTC."

"You're not alone," Segal said. "But that's the point. A good reporter has to learn to put his personal opinions aside and write objectively."

At the time, UCLA was mandated by the state to enroll its male students in the ROTC program. I satisfied the requirement by donning a uniform and striding up and down the football field three times a week with my saxophone, doing my best not to fall out of step while we played a medley of military marches. I declined the extracurricular options of target practice and learning how to dismantle and reassemble an M1 Garand rifle.

"ROTC is nothing but political indoctrination," I protested to Segal.

"You can leave that out," he replied. "Deadline in two days."

The next day, I was ushered into the spacious office of Colonel Moore. He was a trim looking figure whose advancing age had done little to alter his military bearing.

"Please, have a chair, Mr. Goldbrick."

"Goldman," I corrected.

"Yes," he said, gesturing to one of the spindle-backed chairs emblazoned with the university seal. "I'm told you're writing a history of our program."

His courtly manner and leisurely vowels hinted at the Alabama background my research had revealed.

"Well, it's more like a feature story for *The Daily Bruin*."

"Ah yes, the student newspaper," he said.

"I was hoping you could give me a tour of the facilities and talk a little about your objectives," I said, not certain if he was aware of the paper's liberal reputation that had already created numerous tensions with the university's administration.

"Certainly, Mr. Goldbin," he said, rising from his chair and towering above me. "I'd be happy to."

For the next hour, Colonel Moore explained the history of the numerous trophies on display in the glass-fronted cabinets that lined his office. In a modest tone, he also talked about having come from a military family that had served in every major conflict, starting with the American Revolution. I refrained from asking about their participation in the Civil War. Toward the end of the interview, as I was about to close my notepad, Colonel Moore said there was one other point I might find interesting.

"What would that be?" I inquired, only half curious.

"Well, for some time, I have been conducting a study seeking to identify those cadets whose behavior habitually—I have come to believe, congenitally—challenges our values."

"Congenitally?" I asked, quickly flipping over my notebook. "Do you mind explaining?"

"Not at all." He walked over to a file cabinet and pulled out several drawers of index cards. "Over the many years I have had the privilege of occupying this office, I have kept notes on those cadets who are disposed to flaunt military regulations. They are habitually late to classes and when they do show up, more likely than not, they have neglected to shine their shoes, or their uniforms are wrinkled, and I won't even mention their chin stubble and untrimmed haircuts. But the really interesting thing is that these students—who tarnish the word cadets—tend to share a common heritage."

"Fascinating," I said, furiously taking notes. "And what heritage is that?"

"Jews," he replied, as though it were self-evident. I could feel the hair on the back of my neck bristle.

"But don't get me wrong," he hastened to explain. "Not all Jews, you understand."

"Oh?" I couldn't help thinking that Segal was not going to believe this.

"No," Colonel Moore continued. "My research has demonstrated that it is primarily the subset of Hungo-Slovakian Jews who display these tendencies."

"Hungo-Slovakian?" I tried to maintain a tone of impartial inquiry.

"Yes, specifically those whose families originate in those regions."

My hands were trembling. "And how were you able to determine all this?"

"Statistically. One thing you learn in the military is that statistics never lie."

As I finished taking my notes, I imagined, once again, Segal's scornful response. Then an idea occurred to me.

"Oh, by the way, Colonel Moore. I wonder if you could take another moment to read through my notes, make any corrections, and sign your approval at the end. It's just standard journalistic procedure."

"Be happy to," he replied graciously. He rapidly glanced through my notes, made a few minor corrections in red pencil, and signed them with a flourish at the end: Approved Col. Wiley T. Moore.

"I look forward to reading your story, Mr. Goldsmith," he said, as he held the door for me.

"Certainly, I'll bring you a copy before the ink dries," I said, not bothering to correct his mispronunciation of my name.

I stayed up past midnight typing the story. When I handed it to Segal the next morning, an angry flush suffused his face as he read it.

"You made this up, Goldman" he growled. "I should have expected something like this." He slammed the typed copy onto his desk. I waited a moment, then I produced my notes with Colonel Moore's bold signature at the end. Segal's eyes widened. For a moment, he didn't know what to say. Then he took a deep breath.

"We still can't print this," he rasped.

"Why not?" As you can see, the story's accurate. I didn't put words in his mouth."

"That's not the point," he declared somewhat wearily. "This story is more likely to shut us down than harm ROTC. You don't seem to understand the politics at the Chancellor's office. The administrators there may not like Senator McCarthy, but they're certainly afraid of him."

"Well, I guess that places you among the cowards," I said, somewhat officiously.

Segal gave me a hard look and thought for a moment. "I'll tell you what. If you can determine that Colonel Moore's statistics are anything more than some kind of weird hobby and that he has ever actually harmed any Jewish cadets, we might be able to go with that."

The next day, I made up an excuse to clear up a few minor points with Colonel Moore. It soon became evident that he had never attempted to go beyond the usual reprimands with the "Hungo-Slovakian" cadets. As I left his office, I mumbled something about how the story might be indefinitely delayed due to other priorities at *The Bruin*.

"Well, I'd be surely disappointed, Mr. Goldbrick," he said.

Despite his refusal to publish my ROTC story, Segal's worst fears were soon justified when the Cal State Chancellor used the excuse of preventing political bias, to announce that the Bruin's editor, managing editor and feature editor would no longer be chosen by the paper's staff but by the election of the entire student body—even though it was plain that most students didn't know the difference among those positions and couldn't care less.

In response, *The Bruin* staff went out on strike and staged a mock funeral for the paper. Segal and I were among the pallbearers who led a procession of several hundred students carrying placards with hand-lettered slogans like "Hands off *The Daily Bruin*" and "Free Press R.I.P."

"I wish we had published your damn story after all," Segal muttered as we wound through the campus.

Chapter 12

Toward the end of the semester, I was alone in the house studying for my final exams. My brother was at the drive-in restaurant where he worked part time while taking classes at L.A. City College, and my mother had taken eight-year-old Laurie Ann to her ballet lesson. As usual, my father was on the road. Just as I was taking notes on George Eliot's *Middlemarch* for my English exam, the telephone rang. When I answered, I was surprised to hear Uncle Jules' voice, calling from Paris.

"Is that you, Jackie?" he said. "You're just the one I wanted to talk to. How about coming this summer to spend a few weeks with us in Paris? We'd love to show you the sights and maybe you could see the first cut of the new movie I'm making."

For a moment, I thought I was dreaming, but I gladly accepted his invitation. Jules and his family had previously moved to Paris after he was blacklisted in Hollywood for refusing to testify before the House Un-American Activities Committee. With the covert help of Darryl Zanuck, the head of RKO Studios, he had already directed a successful movie in London called *Night and the City*, starring Richard Widmark. After that, he was able to make connections in the French film industry and was directing a low-budget jewelry heist movie based on a French novel called *Rififi*. It didn't hurt that his name, Jules Dassin, sounded French.

To save money, I booked passage from New York to Calais on a refitted World War I hospital ship that offered dormitory rates for students. Instead of cabins, we were crowded in the lower deck on cots that once may have held the casualties of war. After lights out on the first night, there were loud complaints that it was too hot. Someone clambered over the cots in the dark and managed to swing open one of the portholes. We all breathed a sigh of relief. The next morning we discovered that the porthole was double-sided and had remained sealed on the outside.

The food in the mess hall was surprisingly good, though on days when the sea was rough, not everyone could appreciate the efforts of the Portuguese chef. Like me, many of the passengers were young Americans crossing the ocean for the first time. But there were also not a few European students, accustomed to traveling abroad, who looked on the balancing act of us unsteady landlubbers with a certain amount of amusement.

On our last day out, we got the news that Ethel and Julius Rosenberg had been executed at Sing Sing Prison. When she heard what had happened, one of the girls from New York rushed down to the lower deck. A few minutes later, she reappeared with a t-shirt emblazoned with the words: "Save The Rosenbergs." Then she tied the shirt to the jackstaff at the bow of the ship where it flapped in the wind like a defiant flag.

Jules and Bea had a top floor apartment in the Rue du Bac. Together with my cousins, they occupied all the bedrooms, so I was installed a flight above in a low-ceilinged chambre de bonne. On the first day of my visit, I went with Jules and Bea to a corner cafe for lunch. After a meal of croissants and mushroom omelettes, Bea insisted that I have a Bon Chretien pear with a glass of sauterne. I don't think I'll ever forget the intense flavor of that pear.

"How do you like it?" she asked.

I rolled my eyes.

"Welcome to Paris," she said.

Then Jules asked me if I was still involved with Mel Levine's daughter.

"No, she broke it off," I replied, unable to conceal my disappointment.

"Well, you may not realize it, but you were lucky that she walked out on you."

"Lucky? What do you mean?"

"Don't you know that Mel was a rat?"

"A rat?"

"What else would you call him? To save his own skin he fingered me and many others when he testified before the House Un-American Activities Committee. A few of my friends went to jail because of him."

"Sue never told me anything about that."

"Of course not. It's nothing to be proud of. And odds are she would have defended him once you found out. Then what would you have done?"

"I...don't know."

Jules smiled. "Well, I'll give you the benefit of doubt," he said.

"I think that's enough of that," Bea said. "Jackie's here on vacation."

Then she asked me about my future plans, and I told her I'd been reading a lot and thinking about doing some writing myself.

"Let me know if you come up with a good script," Jules said.

Since Jules was busy filming "Rififi", it was not he who "showed me the sights," but Bea and my cousin Joe. For the next couple of weeks, we visited practically every tourist attraction in and around Paris—from Notre Dame and the Louvre to the Left Bank and Versailles. It was awe inspiring and exhausting. But I never confessed to Aunt Bea that my greatest pleasure was when she took us to a matinee of Jacques Tati's comedy, *Les Vacances de Monsieur Hulot*. I practically fell off my seat laughing.

At Bea's suggestion, I enrolled in a summer French course for international students at the Alliance Francaise. After a few days, I became acquainted with a classmate named Luis, the son of a Panamanian embassy official. Unlike me, he was always impeccably dressed with a jacket and tie and polished black loafers. At first, I was put off by his air of savoir vivre, but he seemed friendly enough and, when he offered to give me a lift to class every morning, I accepted. The next morning I found a chauffeured limousine waiting for me at the curb. After that, I wasn't sure if the show of respect afforded me by our fellow students wasn't tinged with mockery.

We had the day off on Bastille Day, and, somewhat to my surprise, Luis suggested that we have a look at an Algerian workers' protest march he had heard about at the embassy. We found a spot in a large crowd in front of a cafe along the parade route from the Place de la Nation to the Bastille. For the first hour, the mood was festive with the marchers singing and shouting slogans and onlookers along the sidewalk clapping to show their support. Then we began to notice mounted police and vans gathering in the side streets. At first, we weren't worried since the demonstrators were entirely peaceful. But as more and more baton-wielding police gathered on foot, murmurs of uneasiness rippled through the crowd and people began to leave. Suddenly, without warning, the police rushed the front ranks of the marchers, flailing at them with their heavy batons. Some of the demonstrators raced to the cafe where we were standing, grabbing the wooden chairs and breaking off the legs to use as cudgels against the flics. People fled in all directions. I saw one heavy-set woman wearing a hijab leading her loudly protesting son away by the ear. Then a Vespa raced by with a young Algerian crouched behind the driver waving a bloody shirt. When we heard gunshots, Luis and I made a dash for the metro.

After hearing my account of the Algerian protest march, Jules suggested that I might want to pay a visit to a leftist writer named Vladimir Pozner he had come to know in Paris. "He wrote a book about a road trip he took in the US back in the '30s as well as a screenplay for a 1944 film called *The Conspirators*, about the Dutch resistance in World War II. We call him Volodya. I think you'll find him interesting."

I found Volodya in a small Left Bank apartment crammed with books and newspapers in French, English and Russian. He had a pale, narrow face and thinning gray hair brushed back from his deeply-lined forehead. "Excuse my untidiness," he said, clearing off a pile of newspapers from the chair he offered me. We chatted about my impressions of Paris, and he nodded when I told him about the Algerian demonstration I had seen. "Yes," he said, "what you saw was another sign of the inevitable collapse of Western colonialism." Then he asked me to tell him about the rise of McCarthyism in the US. Of course, he knew about the Hollywood blacklist and my Uncle Jules.

When he asked me what I had been reading lately, I didn't say *Middlemarch*, but Jack London's *Iron Heel*, and *It Can't Happen Here* by Upton Sinclair. "Sometimes fiction foretells the future better than the newspapers," he declared. "Did you know that Dos Passos once said fascism is so common among Americans that they were immunized against it?" When he asked me where I had gone to school, he showed only mild interest when I told him about the UCLA administration's takeover of *The Daily Bruin*. But he nodded approvingly when I told him about leaving Caltech. "At least you didn't have a chance to invent any new weapons," he said, rising from his chair to indicate our conversation was over.

On one of my last mornings in Paris, Luis directed the driver to take us to a small hotel instead of to school. "I have a surprise for you," he said. When we entered the lobby, two pretty girls, one about my age, rose from the couch and greeted us. Luis, who by this time was more fluent in French than I, appeared to know the older one. After a brief conversation with her, he introduced us.

"Jacques," he said with a wink, "this is my acquaintance Jeanne and her friend Denise. Jeanne and I will be in room 5 and Denise will show you to room 11."

I didn't know if I was more frightened or thrilled when Denise took my hand and led me up two flights of stairs. She must have sensed my inexperience, when after firmly sitting me down on the bed, she rapidly removed her dress and stepped out of her underwear. I was struck by how young she was–barely past her teens, with breasts like two unripe pears. Smiling, she helped me out of my clothes and, with a glance at the clock, pulled me under the covers.

Afterwards, Denise, using sign language and broken English, asked me to walk with her to her apartment because she didn't want to be bothered by any more clients. She was pleased when I agreed to her request in my rudimentary French. As we strolled hand-in-hand like two lovers along one of the side streets in Pigalle, I had the feeling, if only for the moment, that she was treating me like an early boyfriend.

Aunt Bea insisted on booking passage for me on the Queen Mary liner for my return trip. On the boat train to Le Havre it occurred to me that I had forgotten to thank Luis for my rite of passage.

Chapter 13

After returning to UCLA, I went with a few friends to a recital in Royce Hall of one of Schumann's Piano Sonatas by an M.F.A. student named Tania Aginsky. Tania had a thin, almost frail figure and walked with a slight limp, the result, I was told, of a severe bout of childhood polio. It was difficult to believe that the delicate young woman on stage was capable of the powerful performance we were hearing. After the enthusiastic applause, I went backstage with my friends who introduced me to Tania, and she invited us to a party at her home. She lived with her parents in an extended two-story house on Wilcox Place a few blocks from Santa Monica Boulevard. One wing of the house was devoted to her father's medical practice. Tania's mother, a sturdy middle-aged woman with world-weary eyes, met us at the door. Inside, her father beckoned to us to join him at the dining room table where there was a display of Russian delicacies. With the air of an affable family doctor who could do no harm, he began dispensing glasses filled with Russian vodka for a toast to Tania: "To my beautiful and talented daughter whose music helps to heal the world," he smiled at her, swallowing his vodka in a single gulp.

I half-expected the appearance of a balalaika orchestra but had to settle instead for a lecture from Tania's mother, Olga, about McCarthyism and the U.S.-inspired Cold War. She seemed almost disappointed when I politely agreed with her. As she began surveying the room for someone more in need of enlightenment, Tania approached and invited me to sit beside her on the couch. I repeated how much I enjoyed her performance and asked if she intended to pursue a concert career.

"I'm not sure. I've been invited to perform this summer at the Tanglewood Music Festival in Massachusetts. I love playing the piano and even performing, but the life of a concert pianist is another matter. I just don't know if I want to spend the rest of my life living in hotels and becoming a persona rather than a person. Anyway, what kind of music do you like?"

"Oh, all kinds—folk, jazz, classical," I said, vaguely.

To my surprise, she said that she loved jazz and that we should go sometime to a concert at the Lighthouse Cafe in Hermosa Beach. I couldn't help telling her that I played the alto sax in dance bands, but I didn't mention the ROTC marching band.

"Saxophone?" she said. "So that's why you like jazz."

I nodded, and quickly changed the subject.

Somehow, whatever musical limitations Tania may have inferred from my diffidence didn't seem to matter and we began driving in her two-door convertible to jazz clubs and concerts at Philharmonic Hall. It was thrilling for me to attend live performances of music that, for the most part, I had only heard on recordings.

Given the Aginskys' left-wing sympathies, I was not surprised when Tania suggested going to see *Salt of the Earth*, a movie about a hard-fought miners' strike in New Mexico where the miners' wives played a pivotal role. The director, Herbert Biberman, whom I had once heard Uncle Jules call "gutsy", made the film after having been jailed for refusing to testify before the House Un-American Activities Committee. His film had been denounced as communist propaganda and Hollywood studios did their utmost to discourage theaters from screening it. At the small West L.A. movie house which was defying the boycott, we were greeted by a noisy picket line organized by the American Legion. There were shouts of "Better dead than red," and "If you don't like it here, go back to Russia." It was the first time I ever crossed a picket line.

After the movie, Tania suggested that we should drop in on her older sister, Nina, who was living with her boyfriend in a nearby apartment. Nina, she told me, was studying sociology at USC, and her boyfriend, Abe Chayevsky, was finishing his residency in psychiatry. When Nina greeted us at the door, it was hard to believe that she and Tania were sisters. While Tania had a reserved air of self-reflection, Nina was tall, with a ready smile and outgoing manner that quickly put me at ease. When she introduced Abe, his high forehead topped with a remaining strand of dark hair, bushy eyebrows, and brush mustache reminded me of Groucho Marx, a resemblance he knew how to exploit, as I soon learned. When I inquired about his study of psychiatry, he began pacing around the room as he talked, mostly about sex, Bertrand Russell's advocacy of free love, and Wilhelm Reich's orgone therapy.

"We have to free ourselves from the conventional armor that we imagine protects us, but in reality keeps us imprisoned," he declared. "In our society, we imbibe petit bourgeois repression along with our mothers' milk."

I didn't understand half of what he was saying, though it was a performance worthy of applause. But I was not prepared for the finale. Just as I exchanged glances with Tania, suggesting it was time to leave, Abe suddenly plucked a hibiscus blossom from the vase on the table and put it between his teeth. It was clearly a planned move, because, at the same moment, he switched on a recording of "Hernando's Hideaway":

I know a dark secluded place
A place where no one knows your face
A glass of wine, a fast embrace
It's called Hernando's Hideaway
Ole!

Abe then went into a Groucho Marx slither twice around the table, with the hibiscus clenched between his teeth like an exotic cigar. Suddenly, he grabbed our hands and led Tania and me into a dark bedroom. With a wriggle of his eyebrows, he backed out of the room and shut the door. While I was observing this per-

83

formance, Tania had already disrobed and slipped into bed. She whispered to me to join her. I understood that the whole evening had been a setup. Then I decided I didn't care.

In the morning, I called my mother to let her know I was okay. There was a note for Tania on the kitchen table:

Help yourself to eggs and coffee. Hope you took care not to leave a bun in the oven.
Love, Nina

Tania got her M.F.A. in piano performance at the end of the year, and I finished my sophomore term with good grades, but still no clear direction. By this time, we were sleeping together at Nina's apartment almost every weekend. But when Tania suggested that we find our own place, I had to confess that I couldn't' afford it and I wasn't comfortable having her pay our way.

"Don't be such a male chauvinist," she replied, kissing my cheek. "Now that I graduated, I can give enough piano lessons to pay our expenses. And after you graduate, you can make it up to me."

What could I say?

I was apprehensive when we told her parents our plans. To my surprise, they accepted the idea as though it were the most natural arrangement in the world, though I couldn't help noticing an amused glance between them. My father's response was different. It was clear that he thought Tania, who was several years older than me, was robbing the cradle—even though she was paying for it.

We rented an apartment over a backyard garage in West L.A. from an elderly Armenian emigre with sagging shoulders and an arched nose that plunged into his bristly gray mustache.

"My name is Tigran Grigoryan," he introduced himself with a slight bow. "But you can call me Tee. That's what my parrot here calls me." He gestured toward the brightly plumed bird that was eying us from its cage in the kitchen.

"His name is Ari. My wife taught him some words in Armenian before she died," Tee said. "At first I thought he was too noisy, but now, when he says *bari aravot* in the morning, I am reminded of her. Ari, say hello to our new tenants."

"Hello," said the parrot.

Tee nodded approvingly. "You see? He's bilingual."

There was no room in the apartment for Tanya's Steinway, but she told me she could practice and give piano lessons at her parents' house. "My father says the only reason his patients keep coming back is to hear me play."

After I finished packing, I went over to the Richards to say goodbye. When I told them about moving in with Tanya, Olga asked how we could afford it. I told her about Tanya's piano lessons, but to cover my embarrassment, I said I was planning to find a summer job and "maybe taking a leave of absence from UCLA next year."

Olga looked doubtful, but Gene said he had heard that the General Motors assembly plant in South Gate was hiring. "It's hard work, but they pay pretty well," he said. "Besides, it might inspire you to begin writing, like you've mentioned. I've often thought that the auto industry needs a novel like Steinbeck's *Cannery Row*. One thing I can guarantee, you'd be bound to meet some colorful characters, even if you just work there for the summer."

Tania agreed that my working at an auto plant might be an interesting experience while she was away for the summer at Tanglewood. But she made me promise to go back to school in the fall. "Of course, I'll miss you while I'm away," she said. ``But it's an opportunity I can't pass up." I reassured her that I would be fine. "I'll get Tee to show me how to make dolmas," I joked.

Chapter 14

"Only fifty-thousand miles," the used car salesman—"call me Frankie,"—pointed to the gauge. I didn't need his back-slapping familiarity to tell me he was lying about the mileage. Still, the 1947 two-door Plymouth was clean, the tires only half-worn and the engine didn't hiccup. Asking price was $150, but after we ping-ponged the numbers back and forth, Frankie grudgingly accepted $125.

"You're getting a steal," he said.

"I don't want to hear about it," I said. "By the way, Frankie, next time you turn back the mileage, don't set it at a round number." He laughed and gave me the finger as I drove off the lot.

Early the next morning, I drove past the stench of meat packing plants in Vernon to the parking lot of the massive General Motors factory in South Gate where I joined the long line of jobseekers. Once inside the building, we were processed like military recruits, including a medical examination where we were ordered to strip. After some cursory prods and pokes, we were told to get dressed. As far as I could tell, even the skinny kid with a sunken chest was accepted.

"Bet those assholes weren't even doctors," grumbled a beefy middle-aged character, struggling to zipper his pants. A tattooed snake on his arm rippled menacingly.

Sitting next to him on the wooden bench, a biker in a black leather jacket and Doc Martens boots combed back his pomaded hair. "Quityer bellyachin," he grunted. "You got hired, didn't you?"

"Hey, you guys!" shouted a lanky teenager holding a portable transistor radio to his ear. "Don Larsen just pitched himself a perfect game in the World Series!"

Bent over, tying his two-toned wingtips, a black man said in a low voice, "Good for him, but I'm a Dodgers fan."

"You would be," sneered the beefy guy, his face reddening. "On account of Jackie Robinson."

"Yes, sir." The black man straightened up to his muscular six-foot height. "You got a problem with that?"

The biker strode over and planted himself like a traffic cop between them. "Cool it, you two," he said. "You want to get canned before you even start?"

We were instructed to report the next day at 7a.m. for our assignments on the line. Starting pay was $2.15 an hour for a two-month probationary period after which there would be a raise of 15 cents an hour with full benefits and automatic enrollment in the local chapter of the United Auto Workers union.

When I entered the factory floor the next morning, the terrific din of men and machinery in constant motion—clanking chains; the spitting percussion of spot welding; metallic hammering; the high-pitched whine of pneumatic tools; the rumble of forklift trucks; the screech and rattle of railway freight cars as they swayed along rails inside the plant—stunned me like a sharp slap in the face.

A foreman in khaki pants and a pen holder in the pocket of his button-down shirt shouted in my ear to follow him. He led me to the first station on the assembly line where a thin-lipped worker was bolting stamped sheet-metal floor pans to the heavy steel trolleys that were rolling past, pulled by large hooks from below. The foreman explained that the different types of floor pan determined the matrix for the model that would be built up along the line: Buick, Oldsmobile, or Pontiac. Gesturing for the worker to stand aside, the foreman demonstrated how to operate the sequence of pneumatic wrenches attached to flexible rubber hoses that were used to bolt the floor pans and posts to the trolleys. At the pace with which the line was currently moving, the entire operation had to be completed within less than two minutes.

"Get the idea?" the foreman shouted, as he handed me one of the wrenches.

I nodded and proceeded to bolt my thumb to the floor pan. Since I didn't know how to reverse the gun, and the line continued to move, I had to endure not a few wisecracks before the foreman rushed over to free me. Later, I learned that word had spread throughout the plant about "that Jew boy's line dance."

By the time I reached the plant infirmary, my thumb was the size and color of a ripe plum. I did my best to deal with the throbbing pain for almost a half hour before the elderly doctor on duty could see me. His hands had a noticeable tremor when he gave me a shot of novocaine. "You don't want to get too attached to your work around here," he joked. There was no mistaking the smell of brandy on his breath. Then he sent me home with instructions to ice my thumb and take plenty of aspirin. I managed to drive home with my right hand. But when I indicated turns with my left, it must have looked like I was signaling with a red light bulb.

"Maybe you're not cut out for this kind of thing," Tania said, emptying the tray of ice cubes into a bowl.

"Good thing I'm not a pianist," I said.

Since I wasn't yet covered by workers' comp insurance, I decided to drive to work the next morning. This time, the foreman assigned me a job further along the line installing rubber windshield gaskets. An experienced worker was given the task of training me. He greeted me with a look that struck me as both friendly and watchful.

"My name is Jorge," he said. "But if that's too much of a mouthful for you, you can call me George. That's what Clyde there calls me," he said, motioning to the next man down the line.

"That's alright," I said, "Jorge is fine with me".

As one of the half-completed cars rumbled into position, Jorge deftly pressed the flexible rubber strip into place around the perimeter of the windshield. Then he applied a sealant, using a small squeegee in his other hand to wipe away the excess. The entire operation took less than two minutes, by which time the next car rolled into place. Jorge demonstrated the routine for about a half hour. Then he gestured for me to take over. Still clumsy with my swollen thumb, it was all I could do to press the gasket around the glass before another car arrived. Jorge beckoned me to follow as he moved down the line a short distance to complete the operation.

"Esta bien" he said with a warm smile, almost as though he was trying to comfort a small child. "Don't worry, you'll get the hang of it."

Then he quickly introduced me to Clyde, the gaunt-looking worker at the next station.

"What brings you to work at this hellhole?" Clyde shouted, shifting a plug of chewing tobacco lodged in his cheek.

"The money," I replied.

Clyde sized me up. "Well, it won't be long before you go back to school, or something." He squirted an arc of tobacco juice onto the line. "Helps to slow it down," he said, wiping his stained lips with his sleeve.

When the buzzer sounded for lunch everyone froze in mid-motion as the line came to a stop. Lunch break was forty minutes and there was a scramble to retrieve lunch pails and large sheets of cardboard used as mats to sit on the floor. I told Jorge that I'd be right back.

"Gotta pee?" he asked, as he poured some black coffee from his thermos.

"No, I'm going to grab a sandwich from one of the food trucks outside."

He gave me an amused look. "Do you think you're a manager who gets an hour for lunch?".

"What do you mean?"

"Well, you may be a track star, but even so you won't have time to buy something before the line starts up again." He motioned to me to sit down and handed me a generous piece of his tortilla wrap. But the moment I bit into one of the fiery jalapeno peppers, I sprang up and made a dash to the water fountain.

"Si, si," he said. "Now you're a man."

"My father already told me that," I said, brushing the tears from my eyes.

I barely managed a few gulps of coffee before the line started up.

"By the way," I asked Jorge, "what happens if you do have to go to the bathroom?"

"Puedos comer o puedos cagar," he replied. "You can eat or you can…"

"I think I get the drift," I said.

It took me almost a week to master the windshield installation without Jorge's help. Adding insult to injury, men in business suits and ties sometimes hovered over us with stopwatches to time our every motion. At the end of the shift I could barely raise my arms to put on my jacket. One day, I made the mistake of telling Clyde that our repetitive tasks reminded me of Sisyphus. "Sissy Puss, that's you, college boy," he grinned, baring his tobacco-stained teeth.

I wondered why our union, despite its reputation for militancy, seemed ineffectual in the face of the miserable working conditions. In addition to the speedup policy and abbreviated lunch period, there were so few relief men to take our place on the line that workers frequently unzipped and peed on the cars. "It's called a lube job," Jorge told me. Many of the old timers referred to the plant as "The Zoo," and when white-shirted managers appeared on the catwalks above us with visitors touring the factory, men on the line would start scratching their armpits and gibbering like monkeys.

One morning, I witnessed a scuffle at one of the company's suggestion boxes that were scattered around the plant.

"What in Hell do you think you're doing, you dumbass cracker?"

A burly Black welder had grabbed the arm of a young white worker who was about to place the slip he had filled out into the slot.

"You want to help them speed up the line even more so they can throw your fool ass out on the sidewalk? Next time you want to put somethin' in this damn box, make sure it's toilet paper."

I was beginning to worry when Jorge failed to show up for work for a couple of days. When he returned, looking exhausted, I asked if he had been sick.

"Nah, nothing like that," he replied.

"Family problems?"

"You could call it that."

At lunch he told me that his parents and younger sister had been evicted from their home in East L.A.

"Bad landlord?" I asked.

"No. They owned their house. It's where I grew up along with my brothers and sisters. You probably never heard of the Battle of Chavez Ravine."

"Can't say that I have."

"But you have heard of Dodgers Stadium."

"Of course."

"Well, up until a few years ago, Chavez Ravine was a good Chicano neighborhood. You know, working families living the sueno americano."

Jorge went on to tell me how the mayor and "a bunch of cara de mierda developers" had plotted to build the stadium by promising the families they bought out or evicted to replace their homes with modern rent-controlled apartments. But as soon as most of the houses had been bulldozed — "Sorry you poor beaners, we changed our minds, we need the money to put up the new stadium." His parents had been among the few holdouts who refused to budge until last week when they were forcibly removed.

"Couldn't they call the police?"

Jorge snorted. "It was the Sheriff who handcuffed them," he said.

Thinking it might help to cheer him up, I invited Jorge to have a beer with me at the end of our shift, but he declined. I had already heard rumors that he probably had a mistress because of the way he hurried off after work and—unlike most of us who saw it as a perk—refused time-and-a-half overtime. He simply ignored the knowing winks and remarks like "How's the little chiquita?" But this time, seeing his distress, I insisted.

"Can't you spare a half hour?" I asked. Jorge looked at me for a moment.

"Okay, I'll tell you my little secret because I think you'll understand. The reason I don't have time after work is because I'm going to night school."

"That's nothing to be ashamed of."

"Well, it's tricky enough to be a Chicano around here, much less an uppity Chicano."

Jorge told me that this was his second year at L.A. Community College and that he was taking courses in writing and the history of Mexican Americans in California.

"I'm working on a novel about the struggles of my own family," he said.

Jorge's story gave new impetus to my own intentions to write about my experiences at the plant and it occurred to me that I should spend more time at the union hall to get to know more of the men.

Located on Tweedy Boulevard, down the street from the plant, the hall was a concrete block building large enough to accommodate several hundred men. Inside, there was a corner office and, at the far end, a speakers' platform with a podium. Metal folding chairs were stacked against the walls for use at meetings, but most of the time, workers just stopped by to share their grievances or simply to gossip. (After World War II, there were no longer any women working on the line. Those who still worked were mostly office secretaries and not members of the UAW union.)

Sometimes when I stopped at the union hall, I noticed a fellow with a pasty complexion and close-cropped hair handing out flyers that urged people to find salvation in Christ.

"My name is Clifford Chafee," he said to me one day, extending a firm handshake. When I told him my name, he kept hold of my hand and his wire-rimmed glasses seemed to glisten.

"Goldman? You don't happen to be Jewish, do you?"

"That's right. Why do you ask?"

"Well, we don't have many people of the Hebrew persuasion in the plant," he said. "Maybe a few in the front office, but I wouldn't know."

"I'm not sure what you mean by persuasion," I said, removing my hand from his grip.

"Don't get me wrong. I just wanted you to know that we Christians love the Jews."

"You do?"

"Of course we do. Especially now that we have been blessed to witness the return of your people to the Holy Land of Israel, just as the Bible prophesied."

Clifford went on to explain that the establishment of Israel was a sign that the Second Coming of Christ was imminent—perhaps in our lifetimes—and that believers would be lifted up to Heaven. But I was not to worry, because Jews who converted would share in the Uplifting. And it was his privilege—no, his duty—to offer me the opportunity.

"I'll get back to you on that," I said.

"That's fine. And don't you worry about Israel. It's all right here in Ezekiel 36:8-12," he said, tapping the black leather-bound Bible in his hand. "Shall I read it to you?"

"That's okay," I said. "I'll take your word for it."

One morning, I saw a notice on the employee bulletin board

from a worker named Wes Filkins requesting a ride to work from anyone who lived near his home off Washington Boulevard. He needed to hitch a ride because his car had thrown a rod and was in the repair shop. Since I drove by that way every morning, I got in touch with Wes and arranged to pick him up the next morning

He lived with his wife, Leonora, and their two young children in a Black residential neighborhood of 1930s duplexes with well-tended patches of lawn out front. They invited me in for a quick cup of coffee, where I learned that Wes was a welder in the body shop at the plant and Leonora taught music at Jefferson High School. Her widowed mother lived next door and took care of the kids while Wes and Leonora were at work.

"Can't tell you how much I appreciate the ride," Wes said as we set off.

We continued to chat and had just passed the town of Vernon when I heard a siren and saw a motorcycle cop in my rearview mirror, signaling for me to pull over. After I stopped, the cop parked behind us and slowly circled the car, eyeing Wes and me.

"Is something wrong, officer?" I asked when he approached my window.

"I want you both to get out of the car with your hands behind your heads."

We followed his instructions, and he spread-eagled us on either side of the hood. Holding an oversize flashlight in his right hand, he patted us down with his left. Leaving us there, he shined his flashlight inside the car and ran his hand between the cushions. Then he had me walk over and open the trunk.

"Is something wrong?" I repeated.

"You tell me," he said, pointing to the broken left taillight. He wrote out a ticket and indicated that we could go. We let him roar past us on the highway.

"That's funny," I said. "I keep forgetting to fix that light, but I've been driving without it for weeks."

Wes looked at me. "Yeah," he said, "but not with me. We better go after work to get that taillight of yours fixed."

"Right, safety first," I said.

That afternoon, Wes introduced me to "Comrade Bernie," as he called him. "Bernie here has an answer for everything," he said with a grin. "And sometimes he's even right." Bernie laughed and slapped Wes on the shoulder. "Don't listen to this company fink," Bernie said, wagging his finger. I recognized him as a relief man I had seen moving around the line and had already noticed his quick-witted chatter and the way he seemed to know everyone's first names.

"You're pretty new to the neighborhood," he said to me. "I still haven't had the pleasure of letting you take a piss."

Afterward, Wes told me that Bernie was a Communist Party organizer, but that his real talent was singing. "He's not shy about it either. Just ask him and he'll let loose with 'Singin' in the Rain', just like in the movies."

When I got home, I told Tania about my brush with the law. "But don't worry," I said. "I got the taillight fixed."

"Good. But that's not what I'm really worried about."

"What do you mean?"

"Well, I'm still hoping you'll quit that job and go back to school by the time I get back from Tanglewood. I know it's a good experience, but you come home exhausted every day and I don't see you doing much writing. Even on weekends you're too tired to do the things we used to do."

When I mentioned to Wes that I would be on my own for a few weeks while Tania was away, he invited me over for a backyard barbecue at his house.

"I guarantee you've never tasted anything better than my mother-in-law's barbecue sauce," he said. "And maybe I can coax Leonora to play some of her favorite Chopin for you on our new piano."

I arrived with a six-pack of Budweiser and a couple of small gifts for the kids. It turned out that Wes had not over promised. The barbecued ribs and home-baked cornbread were delicious and, after the kids had gone to bed, Leonore's performance of some Chopin etudes made me wish Tania could have heard her. Wes requested Thelonious Monk's "'Round Midnight" for an encore.

Later, over a couple of beers, Wes told me that it was Leonore who had turned his life around. When he was still in his teens, his family had moved from Mississippi to a housing project in Watts. It wasn't long before he joined one of the street gangs — "stealing cars, fighting over turf, stuff like that." He finally ended up in a reform school in Whittier where Leonore's father was a teacher.

"He was strict, but I guess he saw some potential in me, and he started inviting me to Sunday services at his church where I couldn't help noticing his precocious daughter who played piano for the chorus. I was determined to clean up my act and managed to get into the same high school she attended. At first her parents objected, but we started dating and, after her father died of a heart attack, we decided to get married. I wanted to study engineering, but there was no question that she had to get her teaching certificate first, while I would work to support us and her mother. Then the children started coming and I had to continue working. No regrets. I couldn't ask for a better life than the one I have with Leonore and the kids."

When I told Wes about Tania, he was struck by the coincidence that, like Leonore, she was a gifted musician. "She and Leonore will want to compare notes," he said, clinking glasses with me. "Definitely," I agreed, "we have to get together as soon as she gets back from Tanglewood. In the meantime, she wants me to quit the plant and go back to UCLA."

"Smart move," he said, "do it while you can. I'm thinking of night school, myself."

Aside from the carpenters, electricians and machinists who were classified as skilled workers, possibly the most coveted job in the plant was driving a forklift truck. In a kind of forerunner to the present system of just- in- time inventory management, each truck was assigned a portion of the line which it supplied with everything from nuts and bolts to entire engine blocks that came by rail from Detroit. To prevent the line from shutting down, everything depended on the smooth delivery of supplies that were stored in wooden pallets stacked in high columns throughout the plant. Working from the top down, the forklifts removed individual pallets to select the one that was needed. Often a heavy load came close to the weight of the truck itself, causing it to move with a bouncing motion, not unlike a bucking bronco. That image was reinforced by the cowboy hats and boots affected by many of the drivers. These so-called "parts wranglers" were looked on as a privileged group among the workers. So it came as a surprise when I was summoned to the front office and offered the job.

"Must be some Jew manager lookin' out for you," Clyde commented when he heard the news.

A forklift driver named Frank Shaw was assigned the task of training me. He grinned when I showed up wearing the Buck Jones Stetson hat that I had carried around with me, but rarely worn, since the time my pal Norm Sargent had informed me: "ain't no such thing as a Jew cowboy." But Shaw appeared to be more encouraging. "You're gonna' fit right in, pardner," he said, though I wasn't sure if I heard a note of irony.

Once he was satisfied that I understood the various controls on the forklift, Shaw demonstrated how to insert the twin forks into an empty pallet and lift it into position. "I think you've got the hang of it," he said after I followed his instructions. "Now bring me that load of mufflers." He pointed to a pallet midway up one of the columns.

I proceeded to insert the forks into the pallet he indicated. But Shaw had neglected to tell me to first remove the pallet above the one he had designated. As a result the load was heavier than the truck itself and, when I engaged the lift, I found myself riding a bucking bronco ten feet above the ground. A group of drivers soon gathered, whooping and slapping their thighs with their hats.

"Looks like that horse might throw you," Shaw shouted. Then he used his truck to remove the top pallet and ease me down.

"Just a little initiation, sport," he told me.

That was not the end of my misadventures. A few weeks later, I had driven a heavy pan of bolts to a section of the line called the pit where workers installed various parts on the underside of the cars. As I lifted the pan from the truck and was about to place it on a shelf below, I stumbled and fell into the pit with a loud crash. Someone pressed the emergency button to stop the line. Aside from a few bruises, I wasn't hurt, and several workers helped me back up to my truck. One of them slapped me on the shoulder and thanked me for the unscheduled ten-minute break.

"One thing for sure," Wes told me when he heard about my descent into the pit, "you'll be missed around here when you go back to school."

But before I had a chance to register for the next semester at UCLA, a more serious accident at work affected my plans. One of the half-ton trolleys broke loose on the line and crashed into a man installing taillights on the car ahead. Someone hit the emergency button to stop the line and a crowd quickly formed around the injured worker who, having been freed from the steel vice pinning his legs, was writhing in pain on the ground. We were all familiar with accidents caused by the risky coupling of men and machines on the line, but this one was worse than most. While we were waiting for a stretcher, a squad of foremen rushed over, ordering the men to get back to their stations. Tempers flared, someone punched one of the foremen, and the plant guards were called in to break up the fight. The next morning, leaflets were distributed throughout the plant calling for an emergency meeting at the union hall that evening.

When I got to the hall, it was already crowded with men milling around and gathered in small groups engaged in agitated, sometimes heated discussions. Bernie was there, arguing with some of the men I recognized from the fight with the foremen.

"Even if everybody in this hall walked out," Bernie patiently explained, "it wouldn't amount to a rat's ass unless enough join in to actually close down the plant."

"Well, I'm tired of this head down, fanny up shit," a muscular man with a creased forehead and flattened nose replied.

"We all are, Gary," Bernie assured him, "but we have to make sure the union supports what we decide to do."

"Where's Red, anyway?" someone asked.

Vern Collins, the twice-re-elected head of our local UAW 216, had gained the respect of many of the workers for his unflagging representation of their grievances. He was well over six feet tall, with a head of shaggy red hair that had earned him the nickname "Red". Someone said he was on the phone with Walter Reuther, the president of the UAW in Flint, Michigan.

Soon after, Collins strode into the hall and hopped onto the platform at the far end.

"Listen up, everybody," he shouted. The crowd quieted. "Most of you are not going to like what I have to say. But Flint is not going to back any kind of walkout at this time."

"Then we'll just have to go out on our own," one of the workers shouted.

Collins looked at him. "You know I've always fought my hardest for every one of you–white, black, brown, red, yellow–I don't give a damn. But even if the few hundred here walk out—and I doubt it would be that many—management could easily replace you. So you'll go from the picket line to the unemployment line," Collins warned. "There's no point in that, and you know it. So we're just going to have to work through the grievance process. I'm not any happier than you are about it, but without the support of the

International, we haven't got the chance of a snowball in hell."

But despite Collins' pleas, leaflets calling for a wildcat strike were surreptitiously circulated throughout the plant. When I arrived for work the next morning, there were already large groups of men at the front gate with picket signs. Several squad cars from the Southgate police were parked in the street. Many of us did not hesitate to join the picket line, but others lowered their eyes and hurried inside.

Soon a manager in a short-sleeved shirt and tie climbed onto the running board of one of the police cars. "This is an unlawful demonstration on private property," he announced through a bullhorn. "If you do not cease obstructing the entrance to the factory, you may be arrested." Almost as an afterthought, he added: "You certainly will be fired."

Just as someone shouted that the sidewalks were not private property, large numbers of men came streaming out of the plant to join the picket line. The entire building was soon surrounded. For the next few days, spirits were high at the factory gates with men clapping and waving to passing motorists who sometimes honked their horns to show their support. There were a few scuffles with police-escorted scabs entering the factory. And once, a large truck delivering mufflers failed to stop, forcing picketers to scramble out of the way. One worker was knocked to the ground and angry picketers pounded with their fists on the hood of the truck. A few climbed up on the cab, attempting to grab the driver, but he revved his engine and managed to escape.

By the end of the week, it became apparent that the strike had not succeeded in shutting down the plant. A critical number of older workers fearful of losing their pensions, white Southerners opposed to any kind of militancy, and foremen with previous experience on the line (Wes called them "former men"), were able to maintain a steady, albeit reduced, production schedule. We were not the kind of close-knit community depicted– perhaps idealistically– in the movie, *The Salt of the Earth*, Tania and I had gone to see.

Then two union representatives arrived from International headquarters. They spent the afternoon huddled with management in a top-floor office. The next morning, we were summoned to an emergency meeting at the union hall, with only a few token picketers left at the gates. Vern Collins called the crowded meeting to order and introduced the visitors from Flint. The first speaker, a grizzled veteran dressed in a rumpled jacket and loose-fitting tie, looked like he had served his time on the line. Addressing us as brothers, he began with an assurance that, "from Walter Reuther on down" the union shared our anger about working conditions at the plant.

"And it's not just your plant," he declared. "You know, the president of GM, Charlie Wilson, has said that 'What's good for General Motors is good for America.' Well, I say to him: If you know what's good for you, Charlie Wilson, you'd better pay attention to what the workers at South Gate are telling you."

He paused and took a sip of water. "But that said," he continued, "I'm here to ask for your patience and call off the wildcat strike. Every time you look in your pay envelopes, you can see that the UAW has been tireless in bargaining on your behalf. Your health and retirement benefits are among the best of any industry. But we can only take one step at a time. The main thing is to stick together and keep heading in the right direction." There was no applause when he sat down.

Then the other rep stepped to the podium. Younger than his partner and more polished looking in his Hart Schaffner and Marx suit, he could have been mistaken for one of the front office managers.

"I'll be brief," he said, "I want to tell you about the understanding we reached with management yesterday. First, they have agreed to review any legitimate grievances. In that spirit, everyone who returns to work by Monday is assured of his job. Those who choose not to return, will be terminated. In addition, we have their promise in writing that individuals who were active in organizing this unauthorized walkout will not be punished in any way. That's it."

This time there were angry boos when the speaker returned to his seat.

"Is this the kind of crap we get for paying our dues?" someone shouted.

Waving his arms to quiet the crowd, Vern Collins stood up and faced the room.

"Take the deal," he said.

It was not just foremen who welcomed Collins' advice. Though they might not have admitted it, there were plenty of men who were relieved to get their paychecks again. Then there were the so-called skilled workers less affected by issues like speed up and bathroom breaks. Represented by the American Federation of Labor, they were opposed to the strike from the beginning.

Bernie, the Communist Party organizer, explained all this to me a few days later as we were leaving the plant. "Don't look so glum, Jackie boy," he said, "that's just how capitalism works– divide and conquer. Besides, you'll be going back to school soon, right?"

"I'm not sure what I'm going to do."

"You'll figure it out," Bernie said. "And I'll let you in on a little secret. I'm thinking of moving on myself."

"Do you need to get the Party's permission?" I asked.

He shrugged. "You just have to know when the party's over."

About a year later, I heard that Bernie had taken a job in New York writing copy for a Madison Avenue ad agency.

When Tania returned from Tanglewood I was still undecided about my future plans. What forced the issue for me, however, was her almost casual mention that she had slept with one of the musicians at the summer festival. "Nothing serious," she explained.

Maybe I should have listened more closely when that pied piper of sex, Abe Chayevsky, had extolled the libidinous doctrines of Wilhelm Reich and Bertrand Russell. But even though we weren't married, my dismay over what I took to be Tania's confession, seemed genuinely to surprise her.

"I never took you to be some kind of closet Calvinist," she said. "Would it have been better if I had said nothing about Carlos? I didn't want it to be a secret between us. I'm still the same Tania as when I left. Can't you accept that?"

It was more than I could handle. That night I slept fitfully on the couch. In the morning, I told Tania that I had made up my mind. I had decided to quit the factory, but I wasn't going back to UCLA.

"Then what do you plan to do?" she asked.

"I'm not sure, maybe go to New York."

"And what about us?"

"I think I just need to be on my own for a while. It might be a good time for you to pursue your career."

Tania stared at me for a moment. "You know," she said, "I thought we really had something. I'll leave it to you to deal with the apartment."

After Tania had gone, I packed my bags and went into the kitchen to say goodbye to Tee. Ari, the parrot, said "Hajoghut yun."

"It means good luck in Armenian," Tee explained. He allowed me to break the lease and generously refunded the security deposit. Then he shook his head sadly.

"You were such a nice couple," he said.

Chapter 15

Figuring they could use a second car, I sold my old Plymouth to Wes and Leonora for the cost of the new taillight. Wes drove me to the train, and we promised to stay in touch. After tossing and turning for three nights in a coffee-stained coach seat, I lugged my two suitcases to a newspaper stand in Grand Central Station. For a dime a stumpy man, barely visible behind the display of newspapers and magazines, allowed me to check the classifieds in as many dailies as I liked. A fourth-floor furnished room in a building on West 84th Street caught my eye at $40 a month. I bought a Baby Ruth candy bar and asked the stand operator for directions on the subway.

"Be careful," he said when he saw the address, "that place was once haunted."

"What do you mean?"

His owl eyes widened. "I used to live in that neighborhood and people whispered that the ghost of Edgar Allan Poe sometimes appeared in the stairwell of that building."

"How did they know it was Poe?"

"How should I know? It was a mystery."

"You could be a writer yourself," I laughed.

I didn't see any ravens when I located the worn brownstone on the Upper West Side, though there was a black cat dozing on the super's windowsill. When I rang the bell, I could hear some voices speaking in what I thought was Italian. There was a scraping of chairs and, a moment later, a sturdily built man in a sleeveless undershirt answered the door. A stained napkin was tucked under his stubbly chin. Before I could say anything, he sized me up and asked if I had come about the room for rent. A small child ran up and clung to his pants and I could see several people seated around a table in the kitchen.

"I'm sorry if I interrupted your lunch," I said. "My name is Jack."

"Ats'a right," he replied. "I'm Giorgio."

"Giorgio? That's my father's name."

"He's Giorgio, too?"

"Close. Georgie."

He clapped me on the shoulder. "Maybe we related," he laughed. "I get the key."

He insisted on carrying one of my suitcases as he led me up the four flights, past apartments with muffled sounds of music and occasional loud voices within. The pungent aroma of tomato sauce and sharp cheese seeped from under the doors.

"Where you come from?" Giorgio asked as he unlocked the door and gestured for me to enter the room.

"Los Angeles," I replied, setting down my suitcase and catching my breath.

"Los Angeles? Whaddaya know. My kid brother's a waiter at a restaurant in Hollywood, eh…. Miceli's! You been there?"

I told him my high school buddies and I sometimes grabbed a slice at Miceli's after school.

"Pizza de Napoli," he said, touching his fingers to his lips.

"The best," I agreed.

He rolled up the window shade to reveal a small room with a double bed, a nightstand with a tarnished brass lamp, and a plywood wardrobe that protested when I pulled open one of the drawers. In place of a kitchen, there was a narrow Formica counter with a hotplate, a coffee pot and a few cracked cups and plates. A steam radiator beneath the window alternately hissed and clanked. The only sink was in the small bathroom that featured a stall shower, a cloudy mirror, and a pull chain toilet below a wooden tank. But the room was clean and, at $40 a month—$50 if I wanted Giorgio's wife to do my laundry— it was within my budget. Best of all, there was no long-term lease, so I figured it would do until

I found a job and could afford something better.

"Ever hear of Poe?" I asked, as I paid Giorgio the first month's rent.

"Po? Sure, at's a big river up north, Torino to Ferrara," he said, pocketing the cash. "Why you ask?"

Giorgio looked puzzled when I laughed. "Just curious," I said.

While I was unpacking my suitcases, I was startled to hear what sounded like the disembodied voices of men singing in Hebrew or Yiddish. For a moment, I imagined it was some kind of mystical welcome back to New York. Looking down from my window, I saw a brightly lit hall on the ground floor of the adjoining building. A half circle of bearded men in dark suits and yarmulkes, hands on one another's shoulders, were dancing and singing with spirited abandon. As I stared down at them, I had the uncanny feeling that their upturned, ecstatic faces were directed at me alone and they were reminding me to visit my grandmother.

It had been almost five years since I had visited Grandma Lena before my trip to Europe. My grandfather had died the previous year, and my aunts and uncles had all married and moved away. Lena had declined their pleas for her to live with them, saying she was too old to move. The neighborhood had become predominantly Puerto Rican, and she remained the sole Jewish occupant of her building. Goldman's Delicatessen was gone. In its place was a bodega— open 24 hours, seven days a week.

"And the music," my grandmother had complained, cupping her ears with her heavily veined hands, "they play it day and night."

This time, I decided to surprise her and not call ahead. For a moment, when she opened the door, she didn't recognize me.

"Grandma, it's me, Jackie."

Her eyes widened and she took a step backward. "Oy," she exclaimed, slapping her cheek. "What happened? All of a sudden, you're a man."

"So they tell me."

She grabbed my arm and led me along the dimly lit hallway into the kitchen. The stained porcelain sink, monitor top refrigerator, and four-burner gas stove were still as I remembered them. She almost pushed me down into my grandfather's chair next to the Philco radio on the white enamel table. His cane was propped in the corner.

I couldn't help noticing that my grandmother seemed livelier than the last time I had seen her. It didn't take her long to place a cup of hot Sanka before me. But instead of the rugelach I expected, she brought out a plate of flaky puff pastries.

"What's this?" I asked.

"Try it, you'll like it. They call it cosytoes."

I couldn't believe my ears. "Who does?"

"The Porto Ricans. They treat me like their queen. They do my shopping— even kosher chickens. Every day somebody comes by to see how I'm doing."

We chatted for another hour, and she brought out photos of some of the cousins I had never met. "It's a shame you don't know your own family," she said, shaking her head. "Just like your father."

When she cleared the dishes, I could have sworn that she was humming what sounded like a Latin tune under her breath.

It didn't take long for me to find a job with a company called Management Review, located in the basement of a building across from the New York Public Library on 42nd Street. My assignment was to read as many business publications as I could each week and then digest the articles into an abbreviated version for the convenience of busy corporate executives. The pay was barely above minimum wage, suits and ties were mandatory, and the required weekly business lunch with managers was at my own expense. Sitting at my metal desk in the windowless basement, I was too embarrassed to describe my new job in my letters to my G.M. buddies Wes and Jose. I could only imagine Clive's tobacco-squirting response.

Not surprisingly, I continued to check the want ads for something better.

Around this time, I received a letter from my mother with some exciting news. With the help of her brothers who had confidence in her good taste, she and George had opened a dress shop in Brentwood, and they had moved to an apartment not far from Beverly Hills High School, which my talented sister Laurie — "ballet, piano, acting, she's got it all" — would be entering in the fall. The shop was already successful beyond her wildest dreams—some movie stars had become regular customers and she had hired "a lovely girl named Tina" as a sales assistant. Tired of life on the road, George had agreed to become a partner in the business. "You know," she wrote, "he always had a good head for numbers, so he's in charge of the books, leaving me free to deal with customers and keep up on the latest fashions." Though I was not sure whether putting my father in charge of the finances was such a great idea, I was happy for my mother and sent her my congratulations. A couple of months later, I got word from my brother, who had just opened his first law office in the tough city of Compton, that Tina and her boyfriend had introduced George to the pleasures of smoking pot. "But don't worry," Ron told me, "he still prefers Camels."

One Saturday, I saw a notice in the *Times* that a three-masted Russian oceanographic schooner, poetically named the Zarya (Dawn), had docked in New York Harbor on its voyage to measure the magnetic field of the earth. Journalists interested in interviewing the officers were welcome to visit that weekend. As a lark, I decided to see if the press card I had saved from the *Daily Bruin* would get me aboard—It worked. Apparently the Soviet desire to further their campaign of "Peace and Friendship" with the United States encouraged the ship's officers to cast a wide net in the interest of positive publicity.

Once aboard, I made my way to the crowded main cabin where

a long table displayed several large crystal bowls filled with glistening black caviar next to piles of tiny silver spoons and platters of small white pancakes that looked like crepes. Several smartly dressed stewards made sure there was no shortage of shot glasses and bottles of Stolichnaya and Smirnoff vodka. It felt like a scene from *War and Peace*. I had never tasted caviar, but judging by the crush around the table, it looked like something I had to try. As soon as I saw an opening, I made my way to one of the bowls and piled a few of the fish eggs onto one of the crepes. Not knowing what to expect, I wrinkled my nose and almost changed my mind. Seeing my hesitancy, one of the ship's officers standing next to me smiled as I finally gulped down the morsel. Broad-shouldered, with a muscular frame and neatly trimmed reddish beard, he seemed the very picture of a Russian naval officer in his black uniform with silver buttons and gold braid.

"The first time you eat caviar?" he asked, lifting one of the spoons that seemed incongruous in his fleshy hand.

"Yes," I had to admit.

"Beluga—the best," he declared, still savoring his mouthful. "Is like sex," he winked. "The first time, not so sure. After that, you want more. Now take again, but without blini. Just let it melt on tongue."

I tried to follow his instructions, but noticing my lack of enthusiasm, he laughed. "Maybe for you, is not like sex," he said.

I didn't tell him it was more like the teaspoons of cod liver oil Grandma Lena used to force me to swallow as a child while pinching my nose.

"So you're a journalist?" the officer inquired, handing me a glass of vodka.

"That's right," I replied. But not wishing to dwell on the subject, I mentioned that I had also studied chemistry.

"Ah, so you like science," he said. "Then you will understand what my ship is doing."

"I wouldn't mind learning more," I said. I see you are an officer."

He looked amused. "Yes, I am captain– Dmitri," he said.

"I'm Jack."

We shook hands, his swallowing mine in a single gulp.

"So, Mister Jack, have you been on ship before?"

I told him about my voyage to France.

"Ah, a regular sea dog."

"Hardly," I said, "but I have to say your English is very good."

"Spacibo, I read Jack London," he said, looking pleased.

Maybe it was the captain's friendliness or the several shots of vodka I had downed that inspired it, but I had a sudden inspiration. "Do you ever take passengers on your voyages?" I asked. It was a crazy notion, but the thought of spending a few months circumnavigating the globe appealed to me, both as an exciting adventure, and a possible way out of my dull job at Management Review. Who knew where it might lead?

 "If you have a spare bunk, I'd be willing to make myself useful—scrubbing the deck, washing dishes, whatever you need."

He looked at me curiously, as though trying to decide if I was serious. "So you know not only science but hard work?"

Thinking it might appeal to whatever proletarian leanings the officer class might retain, I told him about my experience at General Motors. He swallowed another spoonful of caviar followed by a shot of vodka. Then he straightened his uniform and asked if I could return the following morning when we might discuss the matter further—"unless you go to church."

"That's not a problem," I said.

Taking out a notepad, he asked for my last name.

"Goldman," I said.

For a brief moment his pen hesitated. Then he scribbled something in Russian and handed me the note, saying it was a pass that would allow me to board.

I had a restless night, and arrived at the ship early on Sunday morning. After inspecting my pass, a sailor instructed me to wait. A half hour later, an officer accompanied me to a cabin where the captain was seated behind a table alongside an older, dour looking man in civilian clothes. The captain's previously friendly bearing was now a posture of formal politeness. He introduced his companion as "Mr. Zinoviev," who invited me to take a seat and, without further explanation, began to question me in perfect English.

"So, you are a journalist?" There was a note of almost amused skepticism in Zinoviev's voice.

"Well, I was a reporter for my college newspaper." It felt like a confession.

"And before that, you had one year at Caltech," he said.

It was clear that he had thoroughly researched my background. But who was this guy and why was he suspicious of me?

"Now you work for this Management Review. Not much of a job for someone with your training," he commented dryly.

"I'm looking for something more challenging."

"Maybe you should apply to your government." Zinoviev puckered his thin lips.

All this time, the captain had remained silent, avoiding my puzzled look. Then it struck me that Zinoviev suspected I might be some kind of covert agent assigned to discover whether the scientific mission of the Zarya was a cover for spying activities. It was like a John Buchan novel.

"You know what?" I said, rising from my chair, "I think I've changed my mind. Maybe this wasn't such a good idea after all."

We didn't say goodbye, but as I turned to leave, the captain turned his palms upward and shrugged, as if to say he had nothing to do with my interrogation.

The next time I went to visit Grandma Lena, a young woman answered the door. For a moment I thought I had gone to the wrong apartment, but she seemed to recognize me.

"Grandma was just telling me about your visit," she said, "and now here you are again. I'm your cousin Josie."

"Tressa's daughter?"

"That's right. I don't think we ever met. Anyway, after Grandpa died, I figured, better than sitting shiva with my mother, was to come visit Grandma. She was happy to see me." As we entered the kitchen, Grandma Lena beamed at me. "Can you believe it? Such a pretty girl. And she's going to stay with me for a while."

Surprised, I asked Josie if that was true. She explained that she had just enrolled at the Art Students League on West 57th Street to study painting. "It's a bit of a schlepp, but right now, I can't afford to rent my own place."

When I asked Josie how Tressa was doing, she smiled. "Hard working, as ever," she said. "But she managed to save enough money from her work at the diner to buy a couple of acres next to our house. And now she's gone in with a retired farmer to sell their produce—potatoes, kale, squash, stuff like that—at the local farmers market."

"And they sell enough to make a living?"

She laughed. "Where've you been? People are happy to even pay a bit extra for food that's locally grown without any chemicals."

When I asked if she had worked in the fields with her mother, Josie looked a little sheepish and explained that she had tried, but she soon found that she was not cut out for that kind of thing.

"I'm more the artistic type," she laughed. "But my sister Molly is in her element in boots and overalls. In fact, she just spent six months on a kibbutz in Israel, learning some of their methods."

"Israel?" I said, surprised.

"Surely, you've heard of the place," she said ironically. "You know, the Promised Land and all that. Molly was so enthusiastic that I was almost tempted to go there myself. They have a program called Ulpan where, in exchange for half-time work, you get free room and board and classes in Hebrew."

For the next few days, I found myself daydreaming about Israel at my basement desk. Why was I wasting my time at Management Review? Even if I eventually got a promotion, did I really want to become the Man in the Gray Flannel Suit? Aside from the appeal of adventure, I began to think that living for a while in a totally different culture might help me to find myself in ways that my present situation could never provide. Still, I had trouble making up my mind until something happened one night after I had gone to bed.

I had just fallen asleep, when I felt something moving across my chest. Startled awake, I switched on the lamp and caught a glimpse of a large rat scurrying across the room. Without thinking, I grabbed the book I had been reading and threw it at the creature. It scrambled away and disappeared through the window I had left slightly ajar. "That's it!" I shouted after it. "I'm getting out of here, too."

The next morning, I phoned in sick to Management News and found my way to the Israeli embassy where I inquired about applying for the Ulpan program. The official told me that, due to its popularity, there were not many openings at the time. Then he hesitated.

"It might not be to your liking, but we do have a slot at a kibbutz called Hazorea. It's an old kibbutz in northern Israel that was started by German Jews in 1936. Very left-wing, socialistic—you might almost say communist. Not every American's cup of tea."

"I'll take it," I said.

I didn't tell Giorgio about the rat in my room when I paid him the remainder of the month's rent. "Where you going so sudden?" he asked.

"I'm on my way to Israel."

He nodded. "At'sa your old country, no?"

"Well, it's new to me," I said.

113

Chapter 16

A couple of weeks later, passport and visa in hand, I boarded the Zim Lines passenger ship, Theodor Herzl, bound for Haifa. Most of the passengers on the ship were Israelis returning home after visiting relatives or conducting business in the States. Many greeted me with backslapping approval when they learned I was headed to a kibbutz. I noticed that the women wore little or no makeup and there was not a yarmulke—or even a tie— to be seen among the open-collared men. They seemed the living representatives of a secular, egalitarian society; a country where, as one of my cabin mates bragged, people didn't need to lock their doors. It was taken for granted that they were talking about their own Jewish neighborhoods and, of course, the kibbutzim. No one mentioned the Palestinians.

On the second day out, I met a young married couple, Eli and Florence Heifetz. I learned that Florence was an American with a degree in art history whose articles on Renaissance and Baroque art appeared regularly in scholarly art journals. And Eli, who had just completed his Ph.D. in physics at M.I.T., was headed to a position at the Technion in Haifa. When I told them about Kibbutz Hazorea, Eli exclaimed that it was not far from their apartment in Haifa, and he made me promise to visit them on weekends. "We have a spare bedroom," he said, "and we can show you the city. Florence may not be up to it," he pointed with pride to her visible pregnancy, "but you and I can go on a hike sometime."

When the ship docked at the Greek city of Piraeus, we had time to take the metro to the Acropolis, where Florence took a Polaroid photo of me standing in front of the Parthenon. On the back, I scribbled "Having a wonderful time. Wish you were here," and mailed it to my father.

Tzipi Shaked, an athletic-looking young woman from Hazorea in shorts and a t-shirt, was waiting for me when we arrived at the port of Haifa. I barely had time to say goodbye to Florence and Eli before Tzipi wrangled my duffle bag and herded me to her truck.

"So you're Jack Goldman," she said as we started off.

"That's right."

"Well, not while you're on the kibbutz."

"What do you mean?"

"With us you need a Hebrew name. So I've chosen Uri Zahavi for you. Get used to it."

Then, without waiting for my response, Tzipi began to pepper me with questions about everything from my work experience to my love life.

"Still not married, eh," she said, turning to look at me.

"That's right."

"A good-looking boy like you. Maybe you go the other way, eh?"

I gave her a quizzical look but said nothing.

"Well, half the girls who come for Ulpan, they're looking for a husband. So you better watch out, Uri."

"Maybe you better watch the road," I said.

Instead of the guided tour I expected when we arrived at the kibbutz, Tzipi drove past the main building to a small cabin near a stand of recently planted orange trees.

"Right now, you have the place to yourself," she said, as we entered the cabin. "But they tell me you'll have a roommate from India soon."

"India? I didn't know there were Jews in India."

"Of course there are. Jews are everywhere. Besides, you don't have to be Jewish to come here. We've had all kinds of religious nuts who want to walk in the footsteps of Jesus."

I had just begun my Ulpan work and study schedule when

Michelle, a petite French girl in one of the neighboring cabins came back from picking beans to find her little Scottish Terrier, Coco, lying dead on her doorstep.

"Que s'est-il passe'?" she sobbed, scooping the limp animal into her arms. "Coco est morte, elle est morte," she lamented. I ran outside just as an older woman rushed over to embrace Michelle. "Pauvre creature," she whispered repeatedly, rocking the distraught girl and the dog back and forth in her deeply tanned arms. It was not clear to me whether she meant Michelle or her lifeless pet.

Later, I learned that there were no signs of injury to the dog, so the possibility was ruled out that it had been attacked by one of the jackals whose high-pitched yipping often punctuated the night.

"Any idea what happened to Michelle' dog?" I asked Itzik, a gnome-like man who drove a small wagon collecting garbage from the cabins. "Gift," he replied with a smirk. Gift? It took me a moment to realize he wasn't talking about the dog's death as some kind of present. He was speaking German. And in German, the word Gift means poison. Apparently, Itzik had been annoyed when the dog barked at him on his rounds, so he poisoned it.

I decided to let dead dogs lie, and I never told Michelle about Itzik, though I was pretty sure she suspected what had happened. She was not the only one. When I said something about that poor dog to my Hebrew teacher, Chana, she shrugged and said Michelle should have known that her pet was annoying certain people.

"That doesn't justify murdering the little thing," I objected.

"Murdering?" Chana scoffed. "What do you know from murder? Killing an animal is not murder."

"Why not? It was completely innocent."

"Of course. But what about the little lambs whose chops you like to eat? Are they not innocent? Does that not make you an accomplice to murder?"

I had to concede that Chana had made her point, though my moral misgivings were not strong enough for me to become a vegetarian.

One morning at the break of dawn, I was awakened by a burly, unshaven man who had barged into my cabin without bothering to knock. Alarmed, I sprang out of bed in my underwear. "Get dressed and put these on," he ordered, handing me a pair of rubber hip boots. Thinking it might be an emergency, I asked if there had been a flood. He shook his head. "Then are we going fishing?" I asked. He grinned. "You might call it that," he said. Without further explanation, he led me outside to a truck with a cylindrical plastic tank mounted at the rear. We drove a short distance to what looked like a small bog where he had me help him uncoil a corrugated rubber hose into the oozing mud. Then he handed me a shovel and instructed me to loosen the soil around the mouth of the hose as best I could. The stink was overpowering. I was standing ankle-deep in a backed-up cesspool.

The driver hopped back into his cab and switched on a motorized pump. Then he popped in a cassette of Elvis Presley singing his latest hit, "A Fool Such As I". I watched him lean back and prop his feet on the dashboard. "For this you came from America," he laughed, wagging his hand in time to the music.

Picking tomatoes was my next work assignment on the kibbutz. But, unlike my aborted foray among the Mexican field hands in the Valley, this time I did not suffer a sunstroke. On the contrary, I felt strong and healthy working alongside other young Ulpan students from countries throughout Europe and as far away as South Africa and Australia—Though, of course, this time I wore a hat.

With the exception of those few ulpanists who had come with the intention of remaining, the rest of us shared a casually lighthearted attitude to the idea that learning Hebrew was the first step toward citizenship in Israel. The unspoken consensus was that this taste of pioneer settlement in the recently founded Zionist land was a thrilling adventure, untroubled by complications of which most of us were only dimly aware.

But one morning, we were startled when a military jet flew over the field where we were working. The plane circled around and, with a deafening roar, buzzed overhead not more than thirty feet above the ground, as though it were on a strafing run. To the amusement of our kibbutz instructors, we dove into the dirt. "Don't be scared!" they shouted, "That's just one of our boys having fun." As we brushed ourselves off, we were told that young kibbutzniks formed the majority of fighter pilots in the Israeli Air Force, a source of pride to their parents.

I soon settled into the Ulpan routine: Rise at six in the morning for a quick snack of a roll and coffee in the communal dining hall. Then several hours of work in the fields and orchards, followed by a full breakfast. Back to work until lunch, after which came Hebrew lessons in a bungalow classroom. Our teacher, Chana Steinmetz, was a tall, sinewy woman whose ready wit helped to soften her otherwise imposing military bearing. The only time she spoke in English was on the first day, when she offered a "thumbs up"—did she mean thumbnail? —history of Hazorea.

Briefly alluding to the forcible expulsion of the Palestinians from the area, she described how the kibbutz was founded in 1936 by German members of the Werkleute movement, eager to put into practice their communitarian principles. Except for basic personal possessions, private property was disallowed. Children lived apart from their parents in a separate facility, though family life was encouraged in the evenings and on holidays

"We have a democratically elected board that allocates work assignments based on the equality of men and women.... at least in theory," Chana added. She took a sip of water. "Still," she continued with a smile, "even admirable principles can sometimes be taken too far. Someone had the bright idea that we should have three sets of showers: one for women, another for men, and a third for both sexes if they chose to shower together. As it happened, the third shower was used only by the theoreticians who dreamed up the idea."

I remembered what the consular official in New York had said about its extreme leftism, and wondered if Kibbutz Hazorea was nothing more than a fringe element in Israeli society. That eventually turned out to be the fate of the entire kibbutz movement when it lost its dominant role in the economy due to the rapid rise of urbanization enabled by reparations from guilt-stricken Germany. Even Hazorea, after heated debate, was forced to open a furniture factory that employed wage laborers–mostly Palestinians who were presumably exempted from its egalitarian ideals.

Many of the older generation at Hazorea were German intellectuals for whom settling in Palestine in the 1930s without their books would have been tantamount to leaving their loved ones behind. I sometimes spent evening hours in the kibbutz library, struggling to read the stories of Theodor Fontane and Lion Feuchtwanger in the original German, often to the point of dozing off in one of the comfortable armchairs. Occasionally, I was joined by one of the older kibbutzniks. But, as for the younger generation whose rapid-fire Hebrew remained incomprehensible to me throughout my stay, the library of their parents might just as well have remained in Germany. The same might be said of the classical music concerts performed by aging musicians, where the audience was a gently nodding sea of gray.

I strained my back one afternoon when I fell off a ladder in the kibbutz apple orchard. Though I protested that my injury was not serious, it was decided that someone would drive me to the hospital in Haifa for an x-ray. I found a seat in the waiting room next to an older Palestinian man wearing a cotton keffiyeh. He returned my hello with a friendly nod, signaling that he did not speak English. But when the nurse called his name, he turned to me and, with a big smile, showed me the label on his headdress. It said: Made in North Carolina, U.S.A.

My back injury was diagnosed as nothing more than a mild

strain.

As I was walking to the bus station for my ride back to the kibbutz, a monk wearing a coarse brown cassock blocked my way. Looking directly into my eyes, he said in English, as though pronouncing an edict: "You may think you are Jewish, but you're not." I was too surprised to respond before he disappeared around the corner. Later, when I described the encounter to Chana, she muttered something about mad monks who sometimes escape the monastery. I wasn't satisfied with her explanation.

Occasionally, Arno, one of the older generation kibbutzniks with the weary expression of someone who had seen it all, engaged in conversation with me in the dining hall. Once, he told me that he had fought in the Palmach, an underground fighting force established in 1941 that conducted sabotage and military operations against both the Palestinians and the British colonial government.

"While it was not publicly stated, we understood that the British mandate dividing the land would not satisfy our needs. Many more Palestinians would have to be expelled from their homes and farms in order for Israel to become a Jewish State. Of course, there are some who continue to argue that the Arabs (I noticed that he did not use the word Palestinians) had the right to resist. But it was a struggle for survival on both sides and we had no choice— not for any messianic religious reasons, either—Hitler was reason enough. But now," he paused and took a sip of coffee, "at least some of us think we must recognize our responsibility for what the Arabs call the Nakba."

Arno went on to explain that many of the older generation on the kibbutz had become followers of Martin Buber, the Jerusalem philosopher and author of the influential book *I and Thou*. "Buber warns that Israel is doomed if it becomes just another outpost of Western colonialism in the Middle East. He calls for dialogue between Jews and Arabs leading ultimately to a bi-national state. That's why some of us at Hazorea have tried to learn their language.

We would like to think of the remaining Arabs in the Upper Galilee as citizens of Israel—though, even on the kibbutz, not everyone sees it that way."

When I described Arno's views to Eli Heifetz on one of my visits to Haifa, he shrugged. "Ah, these starry-eyed kibbutzniks," he said, "they believe that you can make nice to people whose fervent wish is for your destruction. Sure, what they say feels good, but we have to be prepared for every eventuality. Don't forget, we are surrounded by hostile Arab countries that, given the chance, would gladly annihilate us." Only months later did I grasp the full implication of Eli's remarks when I learned of his involvement in Israel's secret development of a nuclear weapons facility near the desert city of Dimona.

But before then, when Eli proposed a weeklong trek to the Dead Sea, I eagerly accepted. I did my best to keep up with his long strides as he led the way along obscure trails and footpaths with the confidence of a seasoned scout. Each day, just at the point when the desert heat had drained our energy, Eli managed to find a camping spot at one of the small oases or along the shore of the Jordan River. It turned out to be a glorious adventure: coming to rest each day at sunset under the vibrant colors of the desert sky; fishing in the Jordan River for a campfire supper; and feeling utterly weightless floating on my back in the saltwater buoyancy of the Dead Sea.

One morning, just before dawn, Eli shook my sleeping bag. "Look up", he said. It was a meteor shower that sparkled in the sky like a display of celestial fireworks.

"That's the Perseids meteor shower. Named after Perseus, the only Greek god to have visited ancient Israel."

"Well, he certainly left a beautiful calling card. By the way, what's the Hebrew word for hike?"

"Tee-yool."

"And what's the word for unforgettable?"

A few mornings after my hike with Eli, I was shaving and accidently cut my lip when Tzipi entered my cabin without bothering to knock. She was followed by a gaunt-looking man with a full beard and blonde hair that flowed down over his collar. "Look, he's menstruating," Tzipi cackled, using her finger to wipe the blood from my chin. Pointing to her companion, she said, "Uri, this is Joachim, your roommate from India." Then, with a curious smile, she departed, leaving the door open behind her. Noting my confused look, my new roommate quickly explained that he was not actually from India, but that he had been on a long pilgrimage to that country for the past several years. Though I had already guessed the answer from his accent, I asked where he was from. "Germany," he said.

"Darf Ich Sie zum Frühstück einladen?" I asked, somewhat proud of myself.

"No need for that," he replied. "I'd be happy to go with you for breakfast, but I prefer to speak English while we're here. Maybe a little Hebrew after a while."

When we arrived at the dining hall, I spotted Arno seated at one of the tables and we went over to join him. But, as we approached, Arno hastily picked up his tray and, without a word, made his way to another table across the room. I pretended not to notice, but I couldn't help feeling the hard stares directed our way as Joachim and I sat down. In place of the usual clatter and clamor in the hall, there was only whispered conversation.

Later that day, as I was shoveling out one of the stalls in the dairy barn, Arno approached me. "I'm not here to apologize," he said. "But I feel I owe you an explanation for what happened at breakfast. He probably hasn't told you yet, but your new roommate was a member of the Luftwaffe during the war. Not many of us care to associate with him."

That evening, when I asked Joachim if what Arno had told

me was true, he readily admitted his role as a fighter pilot. "I shot down several allied planes and even strafed ground troops," he said, his blue eyes looking steadily at me. "After the war, unlike most of my family and friends, I couldn't pretend to forget what I had done. So, hoping to somehow acknowledge my guilt, I went on a pilgrimage to India where, after long periods of fasting and meditation, I had the" … he searched for the right word … "epiphany that I had to come to Israel."

Years after I had left Israel, I learned that Joachim had persisted and that he was a nurse in the physiotherapy department of the Nazareth Hospital.

I met Miriam Dollfuss on the morning I had been assigned the unpleasant task of using a curling iron to burn off the sharp tips of roosters' beaks to prevent them from pecking their eyes out in their version of mano a mano battle. She was coming out of the henhouse with a basketful of eggs when she noticed my wrinkled nose. "Doesn't look like you're enjoying yourself," she laughed. "Smells almost as bad as digging out cesspools," I said. She looked puzzled, but I didn't bother to explain.

"I'd guess that you're an American," she said, placing her basket on the ground.

"You'd be right. But I can't guess where you're from."

"St. Gallen, Switzerland. Bet you've never heard of it."

"Right again."

"It's what you Americans would call a '"picturesque"—she indicated quotation marks with her fingers— "town in the Swiss alps with some buildings dating back to the 15th century. But I'm beginning to sound like a tour guide," she laughed. "Anyway, you should visit us sometime and see for yourself."

I was captivated by Miriam's outgoing manner, and it was not long before I abandoned Joachim to sit beside her in the dining hall. Instead of my weekend visits to the Heifetz's in Haifa, I began walking hand in hand with Miriam in the Galilee hills surrounding the kibbutz. She didn't bother to conceal her interest in me and spoke easily about herself and her family.

"I can't recall a harsh word between my parents," she said. "What about yours?"

"I guess you could say that things were a bit more complicated in my family—But didn't you say you have a sister?" I asked, quickly changing the subject.

"My sister, Ruthie, is the gifted one," Miriam replied, without a trace of jealousy. "She's more fluent in languages—French, Italian, even her English is better than mine. And though she's almost three years younger than me, she's already thinking about which university she'd like to attend."

"What about you?"

"I'm more practical minded. I like doing crafts and working with children. Maybe becoming a nursery schoolteacher."

At the time, I'm not sure I fully appreciated how my feeling of ease with Miriam may have been due to her simple acceptance of me with little interrogation of my past. And when we kissed, it was not passion I felt, but a sense of having found a safe harbor after a turbulent journey.

Chapter 17

As the Ulpan program drew to a close, Miriam's suggestion that I might visit St. Gallen became an invitation—with her parents' approval—to accompany her home. When I telephoned my parents to tell them I had been invited to stay with a family in Switzerland, my mother sounded pleased. She said that Miriam sounded like a nice girl and that *Heidi* was one of her favorite children's books. Then my father started yodeling into the phone.

The Dollfuss family lived in a comfortable two-story house nestled on a wooded hillside about a mile above the town square. When I arrived, her father, Gershom, welcomed me in Hebrew, her mother gave me a hug, and Ruthie offered a formal handshake. I was soon installed in an upstairs bedroom with a view of their garden. Miriam had already told me about her father, who owned a small textile factory in the outskirts of the city. An ardent Zionist, he had been active in the resettlement in Switzerland of Jewish concentration camp survivors. In recent times, he helped organize trips for young Jews interested in "making aliyah"—settling— in Israel. A talented amateur painter, his oil painting of a market scene in Jerusalem was on permanent display at the St. Gallen synagogue.

Miriam's mother, Esther, had a degree in design but chose not to pursue a career after she married. Her perpetually rosy cheeks and warm smile might have served as an advertisement for the Bircher muesli breakfast cereal that Ruthie seemed to supplement by nibbling on a biscuit or a piece of chocolate, her nose buried in a book. Gershom punctually returned from his factory at one in the afternoon for Mittagessen, the main meal of the day, after which he took an hour nap before returning to work. Supper was usually a simple meal of bread and soup, after which Gershom would clear the table and wash the dishes. Except for the high holidays, when the whole family accompanied him, Gershom went by himself on Saturday to the St. Gallen synagogue where he was president of the congregation.

Not long after my arrival, a pair of Spanish art historians came to visit the Dollfuss's. They were interested in the original Velazquez portrait that held pride of place above the living room mantelpiece. Miriam had told me that it was her father's proudest investment and that he had been attracted to the 17th-century painter not least because of the Spaniard's Jewish converso lineage. Under Gershom's watchful eye, the visitors approached the painting as though it were a religious object. Carefully removing it from the wall, they placed it on the dining room table where they examined it with a lighted magnifying glass, occasionally exchanging knowing nods and whispered comments in Spanish. Standing somewhat apart, I couldn't help but notice Gershom's increasing impatience with the procedure. When they were finished, the Spaniards–I could have sworn they were walking on tiptoe— restored the painting to its place on the wall. Finally, speaking in a slightly lisping English, one of the experts gravely offered their opinion that the portrait— "in all probability"—was not by the master himself but— "while by no means a forgery"— had been executed by a member of the School of Velazquez. They in no way wished to imply that it lacked historical significance, though they did not wish to offer an opinion as to its value. Their judgment resembled a medical diagnosis that the patient would survive, though impaired.

After the Spaniards departed, Gershom stood for over an hour staring at the painting. Then he removed it from its place of honor and carried it up to the attic. He never mentioned it again and—at least during my stay—the wall over the mantelpiece remained blank.

After I had settled in, Miriam proposed a walk down to the farmer's market in the town square where I had my first taste of the local bratwurst and sauerkraut.

"How do you like it?" she asked.

"It's good," I said, still chewing. "Maybe a little bland."

"Bland?"

"Yeah, I don't think it would pass mustard at a Yankee game. Excuse the bad pun."

"The bun was bad?"

"Never mind," I said, laughing. "This is how wars start."

Ignoring my last remark, Miriam took my arm and led me through town to the Baroque cathedral that housed the Stiftsbibliothek, the world-famous library dating back to the 15th century. Upon entering, we were required to replace our shoes with felt slippers in order to protect the intricately patterned parquet flooring. Along the length of the ground floor, a succession of medieval manuscripts with elaborate calligraphy and miniature illustrations were displayed under glass in waist-high wooden cabinets. Beneath a ceiling drenched in the colors of a Baroque fresco painting, the room was lined with glass-fronted bookcases. A hand-carved balcony curved around the circumference of the second floor. As we slowly made our way around the room, the hushed atmosphere recalled my first visit to the synagogue with my grandfather.

When Miriam and I returned from our walk, Ruthie looked up from her book to ask me what I thought about the Stiftsbibliothek. I said it was awesome, but it was more like a museum than a library. "Well, compared to America, maybe Switzerland itself is a museum," she remarked.

While it remained unstated, it gradually became clear that my stay with the Dollfuss family was open ended. Still, I was surprised when Gershom offered to use his connections to have me enroll in a German language class at the Institut auf dem Rosenberg, an elite boys' school for international students that was a short walk from their home. I had taken a couple of German courses in high school and at UCLA, so the idea appealed to me, and I was enrolled in an intermediate German class taught by Herr Zehren, a Catholic priest. Tall and handsome, with a deep voice and penetrating gray eyes, word had it that, before he became a priest, Zehren had been a cabaret actor in Zurich. True or not, the rumor seemed borne out on the first day of class when he introduced a measure that seemed more theatrical than pedagogical.

After we were seated, Herr Zehren surveyed the room and selected one of the students, a tall Norwegian boy with a crop of blond hair and a shy smile. He motioned for the boy to stand beside him at his desk. Then— with an impressive memory for their multilingual names— he asked each student to introduce himself according to the model he had provided: "Ich heisse...und Ich komme aus ..." Whenever one of the students stumbled over the German pronunciation, Zehren picked up the ruler from his desk and, with a curious smile, thwacked the innocent boy standing beside him. It's not clear what his intention was, but this touch of incongruous sadism soon fostered a sense of solidarity in the class.

One afternoon, Herr Zehren drew me aside after class. "How would you like to be my acolyte at the school Mass?" he asked. He must have sensed that I thought he was joking because he quickly added: "I know you're Jewish, but unless you're observant it doesn't matter. No doubt because I say the Mass in Latin, everyone begins to nod off. So, wearing a white surplice and swinging a beautiful silver censer, you might be a focus that keeps the students awake." I had to bite my tongue to keep from saying, "You've got to be kidding." Instead, to my own surprise, I replied that I would think about it. When I told Miriam about Zehren's proposition, she thought I was crazy to even consider it. Still, she agreed not to tell her parents if I decided to do it "just as a lark."

A few Sundays later, following a brief rehearsal with Herr Zehren, I assumed my best choir boy expression, ringing the little altar bell and swinging the incense-laden censer as my teacher's resonant voice recited the Mass. Once the students had filed out of the chapel row by row, Zehren complimented me on my performance and invited me to join him for lunch at one of the chalet-style inns not far from the school. After a meal of raclette and boiled potatoes washed down with a Hopfenperle beer, we went for a short hike in the woods. It was not long before this became our Sunday afternoon routine.

Almost every evening, Miriam came to keep me company in my room. She would settle into one of the armchairs with her knitting or sewing while I studied my German assignment. Not infrequently, a mutual glance led to a cuddle on my bed. But unlike my romance with Sue Levine, this time I was the one who set the boundaries. Miriam seemed to accept my restraint as a matter of course—a deferment until marriage.

That, too, may have been her parents' expectation, a likelihood I had to admit to myself when I learned that, beyond the usual questions about my past, Miriam's father was conscientiously researching my background. Once, he invited a lawyer friend for supper whose keen interest in me delved beyond my educational background and political interests into my personal life and previous relationships. It was clear that he had been tasked to test my suitability and commitment to marrying Miriam.

Afterward, I was pretty sure that my somewhat vague replies to the lawyer must have disturbed Gershom. I began to feel that the only thing that prevented him from showing me the door was his daughter's unshakable belief that I shared her desire for marriage. But what troubled me more than Gershom's dissatisfaction, was my own nagging sense of bad faith, my inability to share Miriam's commitment. A storm was beginning to gather over my safe harbor.

In early March, after the winter snow had begun to melt and snowdrops and purple crocuses peaked out of the wet leaves on the hillside, Herr Zehren and I resumed our walks. One afternoon, we began to discuss Goethe's novel, *Elective Affinities*, that he had urged me to read.

"With your background in chemistry, it must have had special meaning for you," Zehren said.

"In a way, but the idea that romantic attraction is like the bonding of chemical elements strikes me as a bit too mechanistic," I ventured.

"Yes, but it's really a metaphor that Goethe employs for the conflict between passion and reason. He is trying to show that human emotions may overpower our rational faculties. In other words, our belief in the supremacy of reason may itself be too mechanistic. Haven't you ever felt an overwhelming attraction toward someone?"

"Maybe."

"Well, you'll know it when it happens."

We walked a little further than usual and I had already turned up my collar against the late afternoon chill when Herr Zehren seemed to stumble and fall to his knees. I bent down to help him, but he suddenly embraced my legs and looked up at me with an expression of abject supplication. "Do with me what you will," he moaned. "I wish nothing more than to be your slave." Though it set off alarm bells, I was uncertain of his meaning. Was this pathetic figure groveling at my feet the same person whose intellect and charismatic personality I had come to admire and respect? At first I thought that Zehren may have suffered a stroke. But when he reached up and began to unzip my pants, I broke free from his grasp and began to run. Looking back, I saw that he had stood up and was looking at me with the same peculiar smile I had seen when he thwacked some innocent student at his desk.

I was short of breath when I reached the Dollfuss's house where I ran directly to my room and began to pack. Miriam heard me and, when she saw what I was doing, a look of incomprehension came over her. The color seemed to drain from her face.

"What are you doing?" she cried, clutching my arm.

"I can't explain right now," I said, breaking free from her grasp and continuing to throw my things into my duffle bag. "I have to take the train."

"The train? Where are you going?"

"I don't know, but I'll call you."

Speechless, she allowed me to push past her and I ran out of the house. I made my way into town, past the old houses and the domed synagogue, until I reached the train station. Passengers were boarding a train at the platform. "What is your last stop?" I asked the conductor. He looked at me. "Basel," was the reply. "I'd like a ticket," I said.

It was late evening when I arrived in Basel. My panic had subsided and I began to question my response to Herr Zehren's behavior. Would he have understood if I had helped him to his feet and explained that I did not share his desires? And how was my sudden flight mixed up with my conflicted feelings toward Miriam and her certainty that we would marry? I decided to call her.

"Jack! Where are you?" Miriam said in a tone of dismay mixed with relief that I had called.

"I'm at the train station in Basel."

"Basel? What happened? Why did you run away like that?"

"I can't explain right now…. I just want you to know that none of this is your fault."

I hesitated for a moment, searching for the right words. "But I can't ask you to wait while I try to sort myself out."

"My God," she sobbed. "Just come back and we can talk about whatever it is that's troubling you."

"Miriam, I can't tell you what happened, but it made me realize that I had to leave and that you need to get on with your life."

After a long silence, Miriam whispered, "I don't understand." Then she hung up.

Chapter 18

I made my way to the station cafe and ordered a black coffee and a shot of kirsch. Noting my accent, the waiter inquired where I was from. I told him I was an American tourist, but I didn't mention my visit to St. Gallen.

"Ah so," he replied, "then you must stay for our Fasnacht. It begins tomorrow at four o'clock and lasts for three beautiful days. It's worth getting up early for the Morgestraich in the town square."

"Do you mean four o'clock in the morning?" I asked.

He laughed. "It's worth it. You'll see."

I checked my bag at the station and wandered around the city like a homeless person. I couldn't escape my sense of guilt over the way I had treated Miriam, especially the shock of my sudden departure. This was entirely different from the time I had broken up with Tania whose casual attitudes about sex and marriage, I had always assumed, provided ample resources for her to deal with her disappointment in me.

After a sleepless night wandering the mostly empty streets, I was startled to find a huge crowd standing shoulder to shoulder in the marketplace. Aside from some hushed whispers, they seemed to be waiting in expectant silence. Then, as the tower clock struck four, I began to see twinkling lights floating like fireflies on the surrounding hillsides. As they descended, the sound of piccolos and drums grew louder and the marchers, with flickering lanterns perched on their heads, came into sight led by baton-wielding drum majors. In my exhausted frame of mind, it was like an uncanny dream.

But my mood changed when the crowd began to disperse to nearby cafes for steaming bowls of Basler Mehlsuppe, a bready soup flavored with onions, cheese and wine, the local comfort food of choice against the early morning chill. Later that morning the parade began with brass bands, marching down the main street. Elaborately decorated floats followed, bearing costumed figures wearing masks depicting everything from animals to public personalities unknown to me. Alongside the floats, clowns—called Waggis by the onlookers—wearing masks that looked like the oversize beaks of toucans, raced up and down the parade route tossing confetti and raucous comments at the crowds. Suddenly, one of these clowns ran directly up to me. Poking his long beak in my face, he said in perfect English: "We know you, Jack!" Then, with a cackling laugh, he ran off. I was stunned. I didn't know a soul in Basel, so how could this bizarre figure call me by name? Was it because I looked American and the name Jack was simply a good guess? This was even more mysterious than my encounter with the "mad monk" in Haifa.

Still puzzling over the clown, I decided to leave the parade and start looking for a room to rent so as not to have to spend another night in the streets—though, if I did, it appeared I would have plenty of drunken company. As it happened, I did not have far to go. Along a narrow street winding steeply up from the marketplace, I noticed a sign in the window of an antique shop advertising a room for rent. A small bell tinkled as I entered and a trim looking middle-aged man in a high collar white shirt and neatly pressed trousers removed the eyepiece with which he had been examining an intricately decorated brass scabbard. "Gruezi wohl," he greeted me. I replied in kind, and he immediately detected my accent. "How can I help you?" he said with a slightly uncertain expression that took in my somewhat rumpled appearance. I told him I was an American student on a travel leave from my university and I was looking for a room and a job, possibly at one of Basel's chemical corporations.

Somewhat reassured, he introduced himself as Martin Hauser and invited me to follow him to a neatly maintained bedroom on the second floor. There was a small bathroom and an adjoining kitchen that was shared with the third-floor tenant. The monthly rent was reasonable, assuming I could find a job. And when I returned that evening after retrieving my bag from the train station, I found a vase of irises and a box of chocolates on my bed stand.

Because I remained doubtful of my prospects at any of the chemical companies in Basel, I decided to try something else instead. I didn't have an ear for Schweizerdeutsch, the local dialects with such stark differences that even people from neighboring cantons sometimes had difficulty understanding one another. But my increasing fluency in so-called "High German", commonly used in Swiss-German schools and commerce, allowed me to believe that I could offer private tutoring to Baslers who might wish to improve their English. So I rented a post office box and placed an ad in the *Basler Zeitung* offering my services.

A few days later, I received a reply from a Fritz Benzinger suggesting that we meet for lunch at a well-known hotel restaurant. He would be wearing a white carnation in his lapel. When I arrived, the maître d'hotel directed me to a middle-aged man seated in a booth toward the back of the room. Casually dressed in a jacket and black turtleneck sweater, he half rose from his seat as I approached and gestured for me to sit next to him on the cushioned bench. As we exchanged greetings, I couldn't help noticing his carefully manicured hands. With an air of polite familiarity, he introduced himself simply as a businessman and inquired about my travels and present circumstances. I almost surprised myself when I told him my name was George Mann and that I had already visited Greece and "parts of the Middle East" before arriving in Basel where I planned to remain for a few months.

When the waiter approached, he scarcely bothered to scribble down Benzinger's order of Wienerschnitzel and beer for both of us. During our meal, Benzinger spoke enthusiastically about Theater Basel, where he had season tickets. Just the night before, he had seen a charming performance of Delibes' ballet, *Coppelia*. He said he had an extra ticket for an upcoming performance of Wedekind's *Spring Awakening*, and he would be pleased if I could join him. I readily accepted his invitation. After we had finished our dessert of coffee and plum strudel followed by a brandy, Benzinger waived off my offer to split the check. But when I stood up from the table and asked if he would like to set a date for our first lesson— perhaps over coffee at a simple cafe— his brow furrowed, and he gave me a look of surprise mixed with disappointment. Finally, in a voice tinged with anger, he said, "Das ist es denn?" It took me a moment to grasp his meaning. I heard him ordering another brandy as I left, knowing we would not see each other again.

I had already made up my mind to buy my ticket to New York when I noticed an ad in the *Basler Zeitung* for temporary employment with the Basel Post Office over the Christmas holidays. It was a longshot, but I decided to apply. Apparently, the post office was short-handed and, to my surprise, I was hired. After a few days training, I found myself delivering mail and shouting "Poscht" when I delivered packages to the apartments on my route. Occasionally, someone would come to their door and hand me a Christmas tip of a few francs or a small bar of fragrant hand soap, a lingering vestige of wartime scarcity.

As it happened, my route included the apartment of the psychiatrist and existentialist philosopher, Karl Jaspers, who sometimes nodded in my general direction on his morning stroll. Dressed in a dark suit and wide-brimmed hat, with his hands clasped behind his back, his deliberate pace left no doubt that he was absorbed in deep thought. At UCLA, I had once read part of his *Introduction to Philosophy*, and it struck me as almost unreal to actually encounter the Great Man sauntering along the street. Later, my esteem for him suffered a blow when he spoke out against a referendum to ban nuclear weapons in Switzerland, arguing for their deterrent effect. Despite his efforts, the referendum passed, and Switzerland did not develop nuclear weapons. In any case, my job at the post office was soon at an end and I found myself having to confront more immediate concerns than my admiration and subsequent disappointment with a world-famous philosopher.

With my diminishing hoard of Swiss francs pointing toward an imminent departure from Basel, I decided to try my luck at the Ciba Chemical Company. Once inside the massive building, I found myself wandering down a hallway lined with small offices. As I passed one of the open doors, a man in a white lab coat glanced up from his desk. Seeing my confusion, he motioned for me to approach. I told him I was looking for employment, hastening to add that I had studied chemistry at Caltech. He started to direct me to the employment office, but when I told him my name, he looked at me with renewed interest. Then he said my German was "nicht schlecht" and that he happened to be looking for a lab tech in one of his laboratories. Would I be interested? I could scarcely believe my luck, and eagerly accepted his offer. He accompanied me to the main office where he left me to fill out the necessary papers.

The next day, Doctor Buecher, my new employer, introduced me to my four co-workers, not forgetting the older dishwasher whose scarlet nose marked him as a heavy drinker. Then he showed me the corner of the lab where I was to perform enzyme analysis of samples taken from patients at Basel hospitals. He assumed I knew what he was talking about, and I said nothing to disabuse his confidence.

"Our research library is down the hall, and you'll find that the cafeteria serves excellent lunches for just a few francs. Any questions?"

I said I couldn't think of any and, with that, Buecher left me to my own devices. I could only hope that the resources of the library and, perhaps, a friendly co-worker would help me get started.

Aside from Herr Blaser, the dishwasher (who insisted on a

proper 'Gruezi wohl' from everyone when he entered the lab each morning), two of my co-workers were senior technicians and the third was a young apprentice who was enrolled in a work-study program. Out of courtesy, they spoke to me in a mixture of High German and English. As an American, I was treated as a novelty, peppered with endless questions about everything from Hollywood actresses to Chicago gangsters. I did my best to invent answers that satisfied their movie-fueled imaginations. In return, they were more than willing to lend a helping hand whenever I needed it.

But our cultural differences came into view one day when the apprentice, who did not have cafeteria privileges, opened his lunch pail and took out what looked to me like a large pancake. Noticing my curiosity, he offered me a taste. As I brought the morsel to my lips I was overcome by the rancid odor of spoiled milk.

"Phew!" I exclaimed, "what is this?'

The apprentice laughed. "Not for Americans, I guess. It's toasted cow udder."

Holding my nose, I said "en Gueta", Swiss German for good appetite. The lab techs hooted, and Herr Blaser let loose with one of his beer-fueled farts that the techies insisted could be ignited.

I hadn't seen Doctor Buecher for several weeks when he came to the lab and examined my notes. He declared his satisfaction with my work and, almost as an afterthought, offered to sponsor my application for a five-year visa.

"Once that's approved, we'll pay for your tuition to attend the university part time where you can complete your degree in chemistry."

Who was this man? And why was he my benefactor? It was Herr Blaser who later provided a clue.

After filling out numerous questionnaires, inquiring about everything from my health to my religious beliefs, and standing in several slow-moving lines, my visa was issued. I decided to test the waters at the university by limiting myself to a single course in physical chemistry. It proved to be challenging, both for the science and the technical vocabulary. To my surprise, there were a number of American pre-med students in the class, several of whom were Jewish and had lost patience with quotas at American universities. It was not long before we formed a study group of our own. Since I was somewhat more fluent in German, I served as translator while we tried to work out the science together.

One afternoon around mid-semester, I wandered into a lecture about German-Jewish writers exiled or killed during the Holocaust. Most of the writers were women I had never heard of, such as Else Lasker-Schuler and Dorothea von Schlegel, but whose work, the lecturer insisted, was worthy of worldwide recognition. I began reading some of the poetry and fiction he recommended, and it wasn't long before I began cutting my chemistry class, just as I had at Caltech. When I finally screwed up my courage and confessed to Doctor Buecher, he merely shrugged. "Literature…" he mused, "sometimes I wish I had studied it myself."

The window of my room on Leonhardsgasse overlooked the patio of a two-story house a short distance away. Occasionally, on warm weekend afternoons, I noticed a dark-haired woman who came out to sunbathe in a bikini swimsuit. As I lingered at the window, I made no effort to conceal my curiosity and she began to send me friendly waves. Naturally, I returned her greetings, impressed by her casual immodesty. So I was more intrigued than surprised one afternoon when she signaled with her fingers that I should come downstairs where she would meet me in the street. Dressed in a pink blouse and short blue skirt, she was somewhat older than she had looked at a distance. Nevertheless, she was certainly attractive, with amber cat eyes and combed back dark hair parted in the middle. She introduced herself as Heidi (I didn't believe her, any more than she believed me, when I told her my name was Jack). As we strolled up to the Basel cathedral, I couldn't help noting her seeming lack of interest in my background and—beyond the marriage ring she made no effort to conceal—her reluctance to reveal much about herself. She told me she couldn't stay long but invited me to meet her the next day after work at Solitude Park overlooking the Rhine River.

It was already dusk when we met at the entrance to the park. I had never been there before, but it was evident that Heidi was familiar with the place when she took my hand and led me to a secluded bench, partially hidden by some drooping wisteria trees whose musky fragrance mingled with her light perfume. A moment after we were seated, she leaned over to kiss me and started unzipping my pants. But when I placed my hand on her breast, she pushed it away. Reassuring myself that there were no onlookers, I leaned back and let her have her way.

Afterwards, we strolled back wordlessly to the street where, instead of the parting kiss I expected, Heidi shook my hand as though we had just completed a successful transaction. I asked when we would see each other again, but her noncommittal shrug made it clear that the answer was never. I couldn't help recalling the disappointed businessman's question as I rose to leave him at the restaurant: "Das ist es denn?"

Heidi continued to sunbathe but she no longer returned my wave. Her behavior remained a mystery to me until the day I almost bumped into her coming out of a cafe. She was accompanied by a stern looking older man I took to be her husband. With closely cropped gray hair and dressed in a conservative suit and tie, he was the very model of a Basel banker. His tight grasp on his wife's arm seemed more like a sign of possession than affection. Heidi's eyes were as expressionless as a sleepwalker's. All at once I realized that whatever satisfaction she had derived from our brief encounter had more to do with relieving the grip of her marriage than with any interest in me. She betrayed only the barest flicker of recognition as I stepped aside to let them pass.

One morning, as I was testing a new bioelectric device, Doctor Buecher came into the lab accompanied by a blonde-haired fellow about my age whose athletic build and erect posture seemed oddly out of place. Buecher introduced him as Siegfried Augsberger, who had recently moved to Basel from Munich and would be working with us as a senior technician. After a few days, I began to notice that Siegfried seemed to go out of his way to avoid conversation with me. So I was taken by surprise one afternoon when he invited me to go out for a beer with him after work. Though it felt awkward, I accepted, and he steered me to one of those Bavarian beer halls where the beer is served in hand-painted beer steins, the waiters wear lederhosen, and an accordionist wanders from table to table. Not exactly my favorite atmosphere.

As soon as we were served, Siegfried raised his glass in a toast to "the land of the free and home of the brave." Something about the way he said it made me hesitate, but before I could say anything, he asked me why Americans refer to World War II as the "Good War." I started to say something about defending democracy against dictatorship when he interrupted me.

"Ja, Ja," you righteous Americans." He took a swallow of beer. "But do you know who really defeated us?"

"Tell me."

"Vodka swilling Russian peasants who didn't give a rat's ass for your lofty values."

I started to make a joke about his knowing the English expression "rat's ass".

But, once more, he interrupted me.

"So tell me," he asked, "what is your confession?"

"Confession? Am I guilty of something?"

"Come, come," he said, leaning uncomfortably close. "You know what I mean— Your religion."

At first I thought I had misheard him. What could be more Jewish than the name Goldman? Was he baiting me? Was he drunk? Did he think all Jews had hooked noses?

"I'm Jewish," I said.

"Ah, I thought you would say that. You may even believe so, Jack, but you're wrong." He wagged his finger. "I know a Jew when I see one and you don't look Jewish." With a smirk, he raised his eyebrows: "Maybe a mixup when you were born, and they circumcised you by mistake?"

I thought of the cassocked monk in Haifa. What was it about me that attracted these nutcases? Were they offended that my appearance didn't conform with their prejudices? I decided that I had heard enough. I threw a few coins on the table and, as I stood up to leave, Siegfried grinned and raised his beer stein.

"Sieg Heil!" Siegfried clicked his heels and saluted me as he entered the lab the next morning. What the fuck? I pretended to ignore him while the young apprentice gaped and Herr Blaser farted, almost dropping the glass flask he was about to wash. The other lab techs went about their work as though nothing had happened.

Later, at lunch in the cafeteria, I made a point of avoiding Siegfried. But as I sat down with my tray across the room, he sang out in English loud enough for everyone to hear: "Herr Gold...man, I don't think that sau...sage you're about to eat is ko...sher..."

When Siegfried repeated his Hitler salute the next morning, I could bear it no longer. I lunged across the room and tackled him. The lab techs rushed over and pulled us apart. Then they marched us down the hall to Doctor Buecher's office. After a whispered exchange in the Basler dialect with my co-workers, Buecher turned to me and asked for an explanation of what had happened. He listened carefully to my version. But before I could finish, Siegfried shook his head and laughed: "Einfach ein Witz! It was only a joke!" he exclaimed. Buecher removed his glasses and stared at him for a moment. "If that's the case, Herr Augsberger," he said in English, "I'm afraid the joke is on you. You're fired."

Once things had settled down in the lab, Herr Blaser took me aside. "I'm sure the opinion of a broken-down old drunk doesn't mean much to you, but I thoroughly approve of Doctor Buecher's decision. Even if Siegfried was only making a sick joke, we can't have people acting like Nazis." He wiped his hands on his apron. "But to tell the truth," he hesitated, "I'm surprised that any Jewish person would want to work here."

"What do you mean?"

"Don't you know that Ciba manufactured Zyklon-B, the poison gas the Nazis used in their death camps?"

I took a step back. "No, I didn't. But I thought Switzerland was neutral. How could you do that?"

"We pretended it was just another product. And we closed our eyes as to how the Nazis used it, myself included—even Doctor Buecher."

To my dismay, it occurred to me that what Blaser had revealed may have explained Doctor Buecher's kindness toward me.

Around this time, I heard that my Aunt Bea and Uncle Jules had separated and that he was living with the Greek actress, Melina Mercouri, with whom he had made several films, including the recent comedy hit *Never on Sunday*.

When I called my aunt, she said she had long since gotten over her bitterness over Jules's affair with Melina and had resumed her career as a classical violinist.

"I often play with chamber groups and, to tell the truth, I'm happier than I have been in years."

I mentioned that I was thinking of leaving Basel and she invited me to come visit her and my cousins in Paris.

"By the way," she added, "before you leave you might want to see the production of Bertolt Brecht's *Mother Courage* at the Basel Theater. I'm good friends with Brecht's wife, Helena Weigel, who has the leading role."

I decided to invite a girl I had recently met at a party thrown by one of the lab techs to go with me to see Brecht's play. She called herself Giselle, though she laughingly confessed her given name was Gisella and she was from Schleswig Holstein in northern Germany. A nursing student at Luebeck University, she had taken a semester off and was working as an au pair for one of Basel's banking families.

"I don't really need the money," she told me, "but I figured it was a good way to get a taste of Swiss life—beyond chocolate and fondue."

Maybe it was Giselle's blue eyes or, even more, her habit of brushing back a strand of her blonde hair from her forehead, that reminded me of my childhood crush on Bonnie Nürnberger.

When I called Aunt Bea to tell her how much I enjoyed Helena Weigel's performance, her reply took me by surprise.

"How would you like to go study at Brecht's Berliner Ensemble in East Berlin? I spoke to Helena, and she thought she could find a situation for you at the Theater am Schiffbauerdamm."

It took me only a moment to say I would be thrilled at the chance and Bea promised to call me once the arrangements were set. A couple of weeks later, her call was not what I expected.

"Jackie," she said, "I'm afraid you can't go to East Berlin."

"Why not? Did Helena Weigel change her mind?"

"No. It's not that. You may not yet have heard, but the East Berliners put up a high barbed wire fence closing off their half of the city. They did it practically overnight. And now, they're turning it into a concrete wall with armed guards. Helena was frantic. She told me it's just too dangerous for you to go there now. Even if you somehow managed to get across, you might not be able to come back. She said she wasn't even sure how long the Berliner

Ensemble would continue."

I never did go to the Theater am Schiffbauerdamm.

I continued dating Giselle and had even begun to fantasize about her joining me when I returned to Los Angeles. But before I managed to broach the idea, Giselle learned that her younger brother had been in a car accident, and she felt she was needed at home. As she hurriedly packed, she invited me to visit her in Schleswig Holstein. Her parents had plenty of room and I could stay with them. I agreed to come and Doctor Buecher had no objection to my taking a couple of weeks off.

It was an eight-hour train trip from Basel to Flensburg, the town in northern Schleswig Holstein where Giselle lived. I happened to take with me a novel Miriam's father had given me in St. Gallen: *The Last of The Just,* by the French author André Schwarz-Bart. The blurb on the jacket described the novel as having been partially written while the author was a prisoner in a German concentration camp. It proved to be a harrowing tale about a French schoolboy named Ernie Levy, the last avatar of a mystical lineage of Jewish "Just Men" dating back to the Middle Ages whose righteous lives justify the existence of humanity. Unable to bear the suffering inflicted by the Nazis, Ernie begins to act like a dog. He survives long enough to accompany a trainload of prisoners to the gas chambers at Auschwitz. Not exactly the best choice for my first visit to Germany, but after the first few pages, I couldn't put it down.

Giselle and her father were waiting for me at the station. She had already told me that he was a doctor with a general practice in Flensburg and the surrounding dairy farms. "Heinrich Schulz," he introduced himself with a firm handshake. A bit taller than me, he had a large head with a narrow nose, sunken cheeks, and dark circles under his eyes. As we walked to his Mercedes, I noticed he had a slight limp. Though his tone was affable, he lost no time asking me about myself and my family. He seemed not to notice when Giselle took my arm.

We pulled up at a handsome two-story half-timbered house in a wooded area outside of town. Giselle's mother, Freya, a thin woman with an upright bearing and tied back blonde hair, greeted us at the door. She had just returned from the hospital and was in a good mood, having been told that their son was making a speedy recovery. It was not long before we were seated around the dining room table for a Holsteiner supper of pears, green beans, goose liver, and smoked pork washed down with Luebecker beer. Giselle was seated across the table from me, and I couldn't help noticing Freya's curious glances at me and then, quickly, at her daughter. Before we retired, Heinrich invited me to accompany him the next day when he planned to visit a number of his rural patients.

After an early morning breakfast of bacon, eggs and potatoes, I set off with Heinrich on his rounds. He told me that he would introduce me to his patients as a visiting American medical student. I was soon deeply impressed by Heinrich's commitment to his rural practice. Not only did he make the effort to visit his patients in their homes, but he was able to converse with them in the local Plattdeutsch dialect. While I didn't understand a word, it was clear that their lively conversation went well beyond immediate health problems. I doubted if there were many remaining American doctors who could afford the time to take such interest in the personal concerns of their patients. Since no money changed hands, I wasn't sure about Heinrich's fees. But, at the end of the day, the back seat of his car was filled with jars of preserved fruits and vegetables, even a few sides of cured pork.

On the way back, Heinrich said he had to stop at his brother's house for a few minutes. We entered an unpaved driveway lined on both sides with giant yew trees whose tangled branches formed a gloomy canopy above us. As we approached, I thought we had taken a wrong turn because, instead of a house, we pulled up in front of a stone building with twin turrets, casement windows, and a massive wooden door. Noting my surprise, Heinrich said, "Probably not what you expected. But, for a castle, it's small and it's been in the family for generations."

Dressed in a loden cloth jacket, full length lederhosen, and riding boots, Heinrich's brother, Ulrich, greeted me at the door with a slight nod of his head. He explained that he had just returned from a hunting trip and invited me to look around while he and Heinrich conducted their business. His formal politeness made it clear that he had no interest in me beyond what he had already been told.

Left to myself in the high-ceilinged foyer, I crossed the granite floor to the open door of a room that appeared to be a study. The wood-paneled walls were lined with bookcases filled with gilt titled leather-bound books. There was a leather couch under the window and a few comfortable looking armchairs scattered about. A large mahogany desk stood in the middle of the room. On the desk, there were several framed photographs facing away from me. When I stepped around the desk to have a look, it took me a moment to understand what I was seeing. The black-and-white photos were of Heinrich and his brother in the uniforms of Nazi officers. While Heinrich appears weaponless, Ulrich is shown with a leather shoulder strap and holstered pistol. Next to another photo of him inspecting a line of prisoners with shaved heads was a framed document thanking Hauptmann Ulrich Schulz for his "truer Dienst", his loyal service. It was signed with Hitler's squiggly signature. I had seen enough. My heart racing, I stumbled back into the foyer where Heinrich was already waiting for me, a thin smile flickering around his lips.

Back in the car, Heinrich turned to me. "I wanted you to see those photos because I make no secret about my past. I served as an army doctor on the Eastern Front, and I am not ashamed of the duties I performed. I don't know how much of this Gisela may have told you, but Ulrich and I joined the Nazi party in 1932 because we believed it was Germany's best hope for the future. But war has its own logic and I do regret the cruelty I witnessed—from both sides, by the way."

We drove the rest of the way in silence. That night I had nightmares of Heinrich creeping into my room to inject me with some fatal poison. In the morning, Giselle looked stricken when I told her without explanation that I had to cut my visit short. But Freya seemed unphased by my sudden departure before breakfast.

Giselle drove me to the station, and we promised to write to one another, which we did for a few months, until Giselle thought it best to inform me that she had become engaged to a young surgeon in residence at one of the Flensburg hospitals. Left unsaid was Herr Doktor Heinrich Schulz having been spared the embarrassment of a Jewish son-in-law.

Doctor Buecher accepted my apology for quitting my job with such short notice. "Sometimes things happen that we don't expect," he said. A week later, I shook hands with everybody at the lab, except Herr Blaser, who gave me a tight hug and a parting fart.

The sky was already dark, and it had started to snow when the taxi arrived. On the way to the airport, the cab driver told me it was his fondest wish to visit America someday. "Such an exciting country, compared to us boring Swiss," he said.

The service on the Lufthansa flight was polite and efficient. And, after a surprisingly good evening meal, many of the passengers had settled back in their seats, reading or napping. We were already well over the dark waters of the Atlantic when a crackling voice came over the intercom.

"Ladies and gentlemen, may I have your attention. This is your captain speaking. I have just received the terrible news that the President of the United States, John F. Kennedy, has been assassinated. Es tut mir sehr leid."

A moment of shocked silence was followed by gasps and scattered sobbing. Several passengers rose from their seats and began to shuffle aimlessly in the aisle. Suddenly, the plane began to shake, causing some of them to momentarily lose their balance. Then the captain ordered everyone to return to their seats and fasten their safety belts.

"We are expecting some turbulence ahead," he warned.

Chapter 19

I almost didn't recognize my sister Laurie when she greeted me at the airport with a tearful hug. "You heard the news?" she cried. I said I had and asked if they knew who shot the President.

"Yes, they arrested some ex-marine named Oswald."

"A marine? Do they know why he did it?"

"I'm not sure. But Dad says there's no way he could have done it on his own."

"Sounds like Dad."

When I asked how Mom and Dad were doing, Laurie said they seemed happy running Mom's dress shop. "I think it may be the first time they really did anything together. Dad figured out the design of the store and does the bookkeeping, leaving Mom free to take care of the customers." I said I was looking forward to seeing them, but Laurie offered to have me stay with her for the night.

"I can smuggle you into my dorm room at UCLA," she said with a smile.

"UCLA?" I stepped back to look at my kid sister again.

"I guess you didn't know. This is my first semester and I'm majoring in Theater Arts. I already have a small part in our performance of Ibsen's *Wild Duck*."

I continued to look at her in disbelief.

"Don't worry," she laughed, "I don't play the duck."

"Well, I'll be a…., as we used to say in the Old West. At this rate, you're going to graduate from college before I do."

The next day, I went to see my parents at the dress shop—"boutique"—my father corrected me, raising a haughty eyebrow. My mother gave me a big hug and then held me at arm's length to get a better look. Except for some gray hair, she still could have passed as my older sister. She insisted that I stay with them instead of in

Laurie's cramped dorm room.

"At least with us, you won't have to sneak into the toilet," my father said.

They introduced me to Tina, the shop assistant, an alert looking brunette, elegantly dressed in a charcoal pants suit. There was little time to chat before both she and my mother were busy attending to their obviously affluent—and pampered— clientele. We agreed to meet for supper at a local bistro along with Laurie and her boyfriend, Irv.

"I think you'll like him," my father said. "He's very tall, very serious, and very intelligent. Knows Greek and Latin. I told him, that—and a five-spot—would get him the haircut he needs."

That evening, I found that Irv's self-deprecating humor more than compensated for his knowledge of ancient languages. My father winked at me when Laurie seemed to stand on tiptoes in his embrace.

"Good thing she studied ballet," he whispered.

A few days later, after turning down several disappointing—and a few disgusting— rooms for rent, I got lucky and found a furnished apartment only a block from the ocean in Santa Monica. The landlady of the two-story 1920s Craftsman-style house was Mrs. Markovic, an elderly Yugoslavian widow. She had been the last holdout against the recent development of high-rise buildings that lined the rest of the street. The comfortably furnished three room apartment had a full kitchen, an old-fashioned tiled bathroom with a clawfoot tub, and even a fireplace in the living room. "Only for show and tell," Mrs. Markovic pointed to the chimney. "Sometimes birds fall down," she said. For a small surcharge, she offered to clean the ground-floor apartment once a week. It felt like moving in with one of my grandmothers.

Still uncertain about my major, I was able to use my previous credits to enroll in the spring semester as a junior at UCLA.

But when I learned that Walter Muschg, the very same professor whose literature class I had audited in Basel, was a visiting lecturer at the Westwood campus, I took it as a sign and decided to major in German Literature. In addition to several courses I had taken on 19th-century German poetry and fiction, I had already read Brecht's plays and it was Herr Zillich who introduced me to the work of Thomas Mann on our walks in St. Gallen when he praised the "sensitive portrayal" of the central character, Gustav von Aschenbach, in *Death in Venice*. So I took it as another happy coincidence that, ten years earlier, both Mann and Brecht had strolled on the same path along Ocean Avenue where I now walked almost every morning.

"That's a nice dog you have," I said to the girl I had noticed several times before on my walks. She was tall, with jet black curls and dark eyebrows that looked like raised curtains over her green eyes.

"Yes, he's a purebred poodle," she replied. "His name is Niko, but he's my father's dog. I just walk him when my father is away."

"This is not a come on," I said, "but now that we're talking, I have the feeling I've seen you before. Not just on these walks."

"That doesn't surprise me, Jack."

"What? ...You know my name?"

"Sure. And I also know that you live in a house on San Vicente Boulevard."

I was dumbstruck. "What are you, some kind of spy?"

"Hardly," she laughed. "My name is Gail, and I'm a teller at the Santa Monica Savings Bank where you have an account. That's how I recognized you."

"So that's it," I said, breathing a sigh of relief. "I've got to say, for a minute you had me going."

"Just like Niko," she laughed, bending down to scoop up the dog's poop.

After that we began walking together whenever Gail had her

151

father's dog.

One morning Gail told me her father was an accountant at a government research lab. "It's a step up from his previous job at the Santa Monica Bank, even though he's low man on the totem pole, working for a bunch of scientists and engineers. All very hush hush," Gail explained. "Anyhow, he likes to go out to the test site at Yucca Flats in Nevada whenever they set off a bomb. He says it's awe inspiring. I've never gone, but I'm sure I can get you an invitation if you're interested."

"Thanks, but I think I'll take a raincheck on that."

As we got to know each other, Gail confided in me that her parents' recent divorce had embittered her father. "He's taken it really hard," she said, "and it makes it difficult for me to be with him. I think he sees too much of my mother in me. The one thing that's kept me going is the Swedenborgian study group I joined a year ago."

"Sweden what?" I asked.

"You must have heard of the Swedenborgian Church."

"Can't say it rings a bell."

"Ha ha. Anyway, Emanuel Swedenborg was an 18th-century scientist, philosopher and theologian."

"Quite a guy. Bet he could run the 440."

"What?"

"Nothing, just talking to myself."

"Well, Swedenborg's teachings on love and compassion have inspired thousands of people throughout the world. There's even a Swedenborgian church near here in Palos Verdes. It's called the Wayfarers Chapel. You should visit it sometime. It's really beautiful. On second thought, I'll send you an invitation. My boyfriend and I are getting married there next month. I hope you can come."

"Thanks," I said, doing my best to conceal my disappointment. "I'm not sure I can make it. But I'd be glad to walk Niko if you need me."

Chapter 20

A few weeks after the fall semester began, I went to a rally in support of President Johnson against his right-wing Republican challenger, Barry Goldwater. After the rally, we were given petitions to take door to door for people to sign for the Democratic candidate. Somewhat to my annoyance, I was assigned to the Fairfax district.

"That's quite a schlepp for me," I complained. "And I don't even know anyone in that neighborhood."

"Well, now you do," said a dark-haired woman whose bold laughter had previously caught my attention. "I'm Bea Newman and I live a few blocks off Fairfax Boulevard. It's near the Farmers Market. So after we finish petitioning tomorrow, you can take me to lunch."

The next day, Bea said she was only joking about my treating her to lunch.

"Besides, it's Sunday and the Farmers Market will be too crowded. Why don't you come home with me for lunch? My mother makes a potato kugel to die for."

To my surprise, Bea was living with her elderly working-class parents who worked in L.A.'s thriving garment industry. They welcomed me to their modest apartment like the hero of some movie Western who had just ridden into town. (Only later did I learn that Bea had moved back with her parents after a recent divorce.) Her Polish émigré father, Harry, was a master tailor who worked in the showroom of the fashion designer, Rudi Gernreich. He had a store of Yiddish-inflected jokes and selective deafness that served him well whenever he chose to tune out of a situation.

Behind a cheerful mask of deferential modesty, Bea's mother,

Goldie, somewhat younger than her husband and a "mere seamstress", as she put it, was the one who actually ran the show in the family. Though she too was an immigrant from Eastern Europe, she was better educated than Harry and it was clear from whom Bea had inherited her quick intelligence. It was Goldie who urged me to take advantage of her "open door policy" to her home.

The first time Harry took me to lunch at a Jewish vegetarian restaurant, he asked me if I knew what *cholent* was. He explained that it was the Yiddish word for the meal prepared in advance of the Orthodox Sabbath when cooking is prohibited. He told me that, in the Polish shtetl he came from, *cholent* was usually a stew of leftover beef flanken, potatoes, onions and beans that was slow cooked in a clay pot and kept warm overnight in a shallow hole. Since the use of tools is forbidden on the Sabbath, the pot was dug up by hand. Harry wrinkled his nose. "But do you think Harry would eat that *chazerai*," he asked. "Never!"

One Sunday, Harry invited me to visit him at work on the following day. "Make sure to come at two o'clock," is all he would say. I climbed the wooden stairs to the Gernreich showroom at the appointed hour and found Harry kneeling behind the back of a shapely blonde, with some pins between his lips. He winked when he saw me enter and continued to fit his curvaceous client in a form-fitting gown. When he motioned with his hand for her to turn, it took me a moment to recognize her—none other than Marilyn Monroe. As he turned her back around, Harry plucked a pin from his mouth and pretended to stick it in one of her seductively rounded buttocks. I had to sneak out the door so I could laugh.

A few days after final exams, I had to go to the hospital for an emergency hernia operation. The next morning, Goldie showed up with a pot of homemade chicken soup. "Jewish penicillin," she said, as the aroma filled the room. How could I resist? I was already the designated son-in-law even before Bea and I got married in a modest City Hall ceremony with Goldie and my sister in attendance. My parents sent their congratulations from Honolulu, where they were taking their first ever vacation, along with a $500 check.

Late that summer, armed with my Woodrow Wilson fellowship and teaching assistantships for both Bea and myself, we set off for Cornell University in the brand-new Volkswagen Bug Harry and Goldie had given us as a wedding present. There was no radio in the car, so while I did most of the driving, Bea read aloud from D. H. Lawrence's *Sons and Lovers,* a novel she planned to teach in the fall. Every once in a while, she pointed out some literary or historical reference in the story of which I was only dimly, if at all, aware.

Bea had just begun to comment on the complicated relationship between the central character and his mother when the sky over Tulsa, Oklahoma suddenly darkened. Lacking a radio, we didn't know what was happening and we grew nervous as we saw the cars ahead of us starting to pull off the highway. Then a police car came speeding by with a loudspeaker barking: "Tornado warning! Get out of your car and lie flat on the ground!" We did as we were told and managed to catch sight of the dark whirlwind—too close for comfort—sweeping up everything in its path.

"Maybe we should have read *The Wizard of Oz,*" I mumbled to Bea.

Chapter 21

The first thing we learned about Ithaca was that it was not connected to an interstate highway. After leaving Buffalo and getting lost on several back roads, it took a folding AAA map and several friendly gas station attendants for us to find ourselves riding along Cayuga Lake to our destination.

We found a parking space in the center of town where we couldn't help noticing the contrast between the two sides of the street. The carefully restored 19th-century facades on one side bravely stood their ground against the opposing row of dime stores, anchored by a two-story Rothschild's Department Store that boasted the only escalator in town.

Next to a candy shop with a peppermint cane sign saying Ban Fluoridation!, we found a smoke shop that lived up to its name, offering everything from chewing tobacco to Havana cigars. Not to be outdone, the news rack ranged from local newspapers to girlie magazines. We paid a dime for a copy of the *Ithaca Journal* and found a listing for a one-bedroom apartment in a private home on a quiet street less than a ten-minute drive from Cornell.

The clerk gave us directions to Northview Road where we pulled into the driveway of a two-story bungalow style house with a large front lawn. A broad-shouldered man wearing a plaid shirt over his baggy pants was mowing the lawn with a wooden handled mower. He tipped a nonexistent hat as we passed by. We were greeted at the door by an elderly woman with neatly trimmed gray hair and a welcoming smile. It may have been the afternoon sunlight reflected by her rimless glasses, but I could have sworn that her light blue eyes actually twinkled.

"I'm Margaret Christie," she said in a high-pitched voice. "I assume you're here about the apartment." After we introduced ourselves as newly hired teaching assistants at Cornell she offered to lead us upstairs.

"By the way" I remarked, "your husband mowing the lawn out there might want to wear a hat on such a sunny day."

"Oh," she replied, turning to look at me. "He's not my husband. That's Mr. Hedges, the handyman from the Episcopal church who kindly does chores for me. My husband, Charles, was the former minister. He passed away last year."

"I'm sorry," I said with some embarrassment.

"No need," she replied. "We had a good life together and it won't be too long before I join him."

"I guess you stepped in it that time" Bea whispered to me.

"I bet she never called him Charlie," I grumbled.

I barely had time to look around the small, but comfortably furnished apartment, before Bea announced, "We'll take it."

"That's fine," Mrs. Christie said. "But you should know there are a few house rules."

"Oh?" I ventured.

"Yes. Number one: No pets, except goldfish.

Number two: No guests after 10p.m.

Number three: No loud music.

Number four: An occasional game of cribbage with the landlady (me) at your convenience. If you don't know how to play, I will be happy to teach you."

"Sounds reasonable," I said.

"One more thing," Mrs. Christie added. "I only have a one car garage, so you'll have to park in the street. But you're welcome to use my shovel."

"Why would we need your shovel?" I asked.

"Oh, I forgot. You're from California. Well, come November, you'll understand."

Bea lost no time introducing herself to the members of the

English Department. She was excited to be a T.A. and looked forward to teaching incoming freshmen. It took a bit longer for the chairman of the German Department to invite me to a "get-to know-you chat" in his office on the ground floor of Goldwin Smith Hall, one of the original 19th-century buildings that formed the Cornell Arts Quad. The building had been named in honor of a wealthy faculty member whose generous donations to the university endowment more than compensated for his well-known anti-semitism.

When I arrived in my only suit and tie, I realized I had overdressed. While the half dozen men seated around the table wore ties —even a couple of bow ties—none wore suits, most favoring tweed jackets with leather-patched elbows. The room smelled of pipe tobacco.

The chairman of the department, Herbert Altman, greeted me with a friendly handshake. His air of inherited authority was heightened by a sloped forehead that swept down from a crop of brushed back white hair like an Alpine slope descending to the crystalline pools of his blue eyes. I learned later that Altman had survived the war as an esteemed professor at Heidelberg University, before joining the Cornell faculty in 1956. Soon after his arrival, his wealthy aunt, Ilse von Cramm, made a substantial donation to fund the construction of a campus residence as a memorial to her son who had been killed in the frozen retreat of the Wehrmacht from the Eastern Front. Altman contributed a short essay to the Cornell University Press publication dedicating Von Cramm Hall that included photos of his proud nephew in his black SS-Obersturmbannführer uniform.

Apparently satisfied with my passing familiarity with writers like Novalis and Kleist, Atman asked me if I had chosen a topic for my Master's thesis. I mentioned Bertolt Brecht as a possibility. There was a noticeable exchange of significant glances. Then, an older professor with a prominent scar on his right cheek, asked me if I knew what Thomas Mann had to say about Brecht. I told him I didn't. He looked out the window for a moment, pausing for dramatic effect. "Mann told his friends that Brecht was 'sehr begabt, leider,' — very talented, unfortunately," he translated, presumably for my benefit. Everyone chuckled in agreement.

Toward the end of the hour, one of the faculty, noting that I had lived in Basel, asked me if I was familiar with the work of the noted Swiss philosopher, Karl Jaspers. "Not really," I replied. "But I did deliver his mail."

After a moment of puzzled silence, punctuated by pipes tapping the ashtrays, Altman pushed back his chair, indicating the end of the meeting. On the way out, he shook my hand once more and told me that the department was pleased to have a fellowship student like myself as one of their teaching assistants.

"It's not every day that we get someone with your background to teach German Literature," he said. At least he didn't say "persuasion", I thought.

By some kind of gentlemen's agreement, sherry and cheese were the ubiquitous refreshments at the faculty parties to which Bea and I were invited before the semester began. With few exceptions, senior professors lived in the exclusive neighborhood known as "The Heights", within a comfortable strolling distance to the Cornell campus. Their spacious homes varied architecturally from imposing Tudor-style mansions to 1950's modern concrete and glass. A few of the parties we attended were catered affairs, but it was clear that the prevailing ethos frowned on the employment of butlers or full-time maids, faculty wives functioning in their stead.

Most of the conversation was about department politics whose incestuous character made it difficult for newcomers to join in, though Bea succeeded more than I. And while there were references to the generally liberal consensus regarding world and national affairs, very little was said about the local community, with the possible exception of zoning issues that might affect property values.

"Aside from plumbers, painters and landscapers, the folks who live downtown might as well be invisible," Bea told me after one of the parties. "And I hate sherry," she added.

Nevertheless, Bea quickly established herself as a valued member of the English Department, popular among both students and faculty. Well before I knew her, she and her former husband, whom she described as her "dope dealer," had more than a passing familiarity with the pleasures of smoking pot. The habit seemed to afford her a point of entry into social circles that I lacked. She found it difficult to accept that my life-long aversion to smoking might account for my disinterest in getting high.

"That doesn't wash,' she said. "Maybe you should see somebody about your childhood hang ups. You're a big boy now."

One thing I couldn't deny, was that pot not only served as recreation for her, but seemed to provide a store of energy she was able to apply to her work. Before the end of our first semester, while I was still indecisive about a topic, Bea had already completed the first chapter of her thesis on Charlotte Brontë.

Thomas Mann might have appreciated the irony when I finally chose him as the subject of my Master's thesis after I had failed to interest my committee in Brecht. But I had no idea of the difficulties I would encounter when, instead of focusing on his earlier works, I chose *Doctor Faustus*, a deeply pessimistic novel loosely based on the Faust legend that Mann had written toward the end of his life. Each time I pursued a critical thread, it seemed to unravel and, toward the end of the semester, I realized that I was out of my depth.

Chapter 22

I had President Lyndon Johnson to thank for rescuing me from my dilemma. His decision to gradually escalate American involvement in the conflict in Vietnam led to the formation of anti-war groups on campuses across the country. Foremost among them was SDS, Students for a Democratic Society, whose manifesto, the Port Huron Statement, was written with the support of the UAW, the union to which I had belonged at General Motors. I soon began skipping classes to attend SDS meetings and to run off leaflets opposing the draft on a young professor's mimeograph machine.

It was not long before I applied for a leave of absence from Cornell. In an attempt to dissuade me, Herbert Altman invited me for a walk along one of the gorge trails near campus. "Jack," he said, "if you go through with it, someday you will look back on this decision as the worst mistake of your life." It was as though he was ventriloquizing my father. Bea agreed to our living on her salary and refrained from telling me that I was "throwing away my life," but she couldn't conceal her dismay.

"Point of order!"

"Not again," groaned one of the students sprawled on the floor of the meeting at Anabel Taylor Hall. "Can't we just take a vote?"

It was clear that the majority did not favor the proposal that we march to ROTC headquarters and smash its many trophies as a way to protest the Vietnam War.

"That kind of action only turns people off," a young woman with cropped hair said.

"We need to figure out how to win people over, not alienate them with pointless violence."

"Smashing a few trophies isn't violence," a lanky fellow in jeans and sandals declared. "It's a symbolic statement that people will understand, especially when it makes all the newspapers."

"I call for a vote!" someone shouted.

"Point of order!"

Despite its immature moments, as the student movement continued to build, some of us decided that an off-campus facility could serve, both as a central SDS headquarters, and a more comfortable location to visit for people with no connection to academia. I volunteered to serve as manager.

With the financial support of liberal faculty, we soon succeeded in renting a vacant store a short walk down the hill from Cornell. We called it The Office and our first few meetings were devoted to plans for rallies and teach-ins on campus. Then Bill Sieverts, whose family was in the printing trade, suggested that we had plenty of room for a press of our own that could print leaflets and posters for the anti-war movement at a number of upstate campuses. He volunteered to run the press for a minimal wage. Once we agreed, Sieverts lost no time locating a used printer for sale at a loft in Buffalo. Eager to get rid of their antiquated equipment, the owners didn't haggle over the low price we offered.

When Sieverts returned with the old barrel press and a camera mounted on wooden rails ("It even has a Zeiss lens!" he announced, triumphantly.), we had to remove the storefront window and use a hoist truck to move the equipment into the space we had rented. In the middle of the operation, with the heavy press dangling in mid-air, our landlord happened to drive by. He almost crashed into the building when he saw what we were doing. But, as long as we continued to pay the rent on time, he never tried to evict us, despite his frequent letters to the *Ithaca Journal* supporting the war.

No one objected to my lettering the name Glad Day Press—a nod to William Blake—on the front window. And a grad student from the Cornell School of Industrial and Labor Relations proposed that we join the "Wobblies," the Industrial Workers of the

World union founded by Eugene Debs and Mother Jones. But, despite the IWW bug on all our publications, no real union shop would have permitted the long hours our motley staff of volunteers put in typing templates, using stick-on letters for headlines, developing photos in our darkroom, and finally shipping the posters and pamphlets we supplied to a growing number of campuses.

One morning, as I was unlocking the front door of the Glad Day Press, I was startled to see a bullseye target glued to the door from which a bullet was dangling by a string. When Bill Sieverts arrived, I showed him what I had found. "Probably some frat boys' idea of a joke," he muttered. But when the same thing happened a few days later, Sieverts decided that it might be a real threat and that we had better take measures to protect ourselves. The next morning he arrived at work carrying a sleeping bag and a Winchester hunting rifle. "I'm going to keep watch for a few nights and, if anyone tries to break in, I won't shoot to kill, but I'll serve notice that they better not mess with us."

"Shouldn't we call the police?" I said.

"So far, all we have to show is a stupid decal. They won't take that seriously. No, the best way is just to scare off these jerks."

Later, I could only speculate that, whoever had been attaching the threatening message on our glass door, had spotted Sieverts sitting on the floor with a rifle cradled in his arms. They never returned. Sieverts had scored a bullseye without firing a shot.

Being somewhat older and possibly less naive than the more radical SDS leaders, I found it difficult to share their belief that our largely white, class-privileged anti-war movement was a precursor to the imminent overthrow of the capitalist system:

"Whaddowe want? Revolooshin! Whendowe want it? Now!"

To my mind, a possible first step toward that desirable, but distant goal, was to form alliances between campus activists and working people in the community. Toward that end, I began to publish and edit a weekly newsletter called *Dateline Ithaca* that focused on such issues as low-income housing, poverty and racial discrimination. We also tried to frame the war as an issue related to those problems, especially for families whose sons were being drafted. The paper was distributed free throughout the city and town, and it was not long before we began receiving letters describing the hardships and sacrifices imposed by the war on the local community—often from the very same people who loudly condemned "unpatriotic" students who resisted the draft, with special contempt for those who publicly burned their draft cards, a political gesture whose consequences most working families could not afford.

"Thanks for the ride, Jackie! See you next week." I had met Mabel Higgins at a meeting of the Ithaca Economic Opportunity Commission that I joined to further my understanding of local politics. Part of President Johnson's War on Poverty, the mandate of the EOC was to determine the extent of local economic hardship, though when it came to solutions, the mandate was vague. Over 80 years old, and the mother of a prominent Ithaca attorney, Mabel had recently moved to Ithaca from Brooklyn where she had been an active member of the Catholic Worker Movement founded by Dorothy Day.

"My son talked me into moving here," Mabel told me. "Walter's rich now and he bought me this fancy condo in Cayuga Heights. He even owns a hotel somewhere on one of those islands. What a disappointment! Who would have imagined that my only son would turn out to be a capitalist?"

When Mabel asked me to give her a ride to the meetings, I readily agreed. It had been many years since anyone called me Jackie.

Another member of the commission was Dessie Johnson, an energetic black woman who worked as a physician's assistant at the hospital. Impatient with what she considered the chairman's politically inspired evasiveness, she was frequently on her feet demanding more effective measures in the predominantly black

South Side. "Hell, the city doesn't maintain the streets and sidewalks there the way they do in the rest of downtown. And when it snows, where are the snowplows?" Dessie liked to poke fun at me over my "romance" with 80-year-old Mabel ... "I don't know if there's anything statutory about it," she said, "but it does raise a few eyebrows."

In the early hours of an April morning in 1969, I was awakened by a call from one of the SDS leaders. "Jack get down here right away." he practically shouted. "Some Black students from the Afro-American Society have occupied Willard Straight Hall to protest a cross-burning at a Black women's co-op. They just ejected a group of frat brothers who came to start a fight and now they've locked the doors. We're going to surround the building to show our support." By the time I arrived, there were reports that police deputies from as far away as Syracuse and Rochester were massing in a downtown parking lot and that the Black students had managed to arm themselves.

Kept informed by some of the SDS leaders, Cornell President, James Perkins, may have headed off a bloodbath when he decided to negotiate with the Black students. The Associated Press photo of their emergence from the building carrying rifles and wearing bandoliers appeared on the front pages of newspapers and magazines throughout the country. Many Cornell professors were outraged by what they called Perkins' "capitulation." Noted literary critic Harold Bloom announced that he would organize a boycott of Cornell "as long as Perkins is president." Bloom soon departed for Yale, perhaps unaware that Perkins would resign at the end of the semester.

Chapter 23

Though my own experience with Catholic priests was–to say the least, problematic—I was nevertheless pleased when Father Daniel Berrigan, the Catholic chaplain at Cornell dropped by the Glad Day Press to introduce himself. His soft-spoken intelligence tinged with ironic humor worked its charm on me, especially when he offered to contribute to some of our publications. It was not long before I was invited to join several others at his apartment for intense discussions accompanied by bottomless glasses of 100 proof Wild Turkey whiskey. A second bottle was required whenever John Reilly, a former colleague of Dan's at Fordham University, showed up. A curly headed leprechaun whose raucous laughter sometimes brought a neighbor's knock on the door, John was Dan's only rival in the Wild Turkey shoot. I wasn't quite sure why, but he and Dan often encouraged me to linger after the others had gone. By that time, the bottle was less than half full and the banter between the two old friends took on a kind of wink- and- a- nod intimacy that was like a code I couldn't decipher.

I felt flattered when Berrigan began to invite me to accompany him on visits to his youngest brother, Jerry, who lived with his wife, Eileen, and their four children in a sprawling ranch house a few miles south of Syracuse. From the moment Dan introduced me, I was immediately welcomed as part of the family. It didn't occur to me that they saw me as more than just another of Dan's friends.

Not long after I came to know him, Dan, along with his younger brother, Philip, a Josephite priest, took part in the theft and burning of draft cards outside the Selective Service office in Catonsville, Maryland. A few months later, they were found guilty for their participation in what came to be known as the Catonsville Nine action. But instead of surrendering themselves to jail, they both decided to "go underground."

In Ithaca we rapidly formed a network of safe houses where Dan could move from night to night in an effort to stay a step ahead of his FBI pursuers. He seemed to take a kind of puckish delight in his technically criminal status and even managed to issue daily cassette recordings encouraging his young acolytes to escalate the anti-war movement by engaging in civil disobedience such as publicly burning their own draft cards.

Under the title "America is Hard to Find", Dan wrote a collection of poems inspired partly by the trial of the Catonsville Nine, but also plumbing more deeply into the spiritual dilemmas of American life. After he read it to a group of us, the enthusiastic response quickly led to a recording with Dan reciting the poems on one side and a rock music version on the other.

But by this time, Dan had grown restless in his restricted role as a fugitive. After a number of Wild Turkey-less discussions in increasingly nervous safe houses, I suggested staging an America is Hard to Find weekend festival where Dan would make a public appearance. Of course, there could be no advance publicity about his participation. So, in the hope of attracting a large crowd, the event would have to be billed as a peace rally featuring nationally known speakers and musicians. As such, we succeeded in securing permission to rent Barton Hall, the largest auditorium on the Cornell campus.

A small group of us met to figure out how we could smuggle Dan into the hall without being detected. We settled on his being driven inside on the back of a motorcycle while wearing a helmet with a smokey visor. But how was he to elude the FBI once he had done speaking? Someone remembered that a group in Vermont called the Bread and Puppet Theater had performed a version of the Last Supper using large papier-mâché masks to represent Christ's disciples. Why not have Dan come on stage during their performance and then disappear from the hall in a disciple's mask?

A car waiting by the stage door would whisk him to safety before his pursuers could react.

"Perfect. Let's see if Dan agrees." I said.

"What about the Jews?" Bernie Levinson piped up.

"The Jews?"

"You heard me. We're talking about the week of Passover and all we've got so far is a Catholic dish-to-pass. What about a seder?"

"I know just your man," said the new director of Cornell's Africana Studies Center. "Ever hear of Arthur Waskow? After Martin Luther King was shot, Waskow wrote what he called the Freedom Seder that draws on Jewish tradition but emphasizes racial justice and the liberation of all oppressed people, not only Jews. I was at the first Freedom Seder in Washington a couple of years ago where I got to know him. I could see if he'd come." Bernie Levinson seconded the idea and we all agreed.

More than ten thousand people attended the weekend event in Barton Hall, many staying overnight in sleeping bags. Of course, there was criticism of the hippie atmosphere where some claimed they could get high by simply taking a deep breath. But the Bread and Puppet Theater's performance of the Last Supper and Rabbi Waskow's Freedom Seder set the tone of moral seriousness that not even the hippies who had come for the rock music could dismiss. As we anticipated, Berrigan's talk was inspiring–perhaps to a fault–when he was repeatedly interrupted by young undergraduates jumping onstage and burning their draft cards with little thought as to the consequences.

The plan for Berrigan's exit as Rabbi Waskow came on stage would have gone smoothly if it had not been for an over-eager member of our group who decided to douse the lights just as Dan was about to leave the hall hidden in a Bread and Puppet mask. That alerted the FBI agents, whose laughable disguises were betrayed by their black patent leather shoes, that the game was afoot. Fortunately, the driver of our escape car was a dairy farmer familiar with the country back roads. He was able to stay ahead of the agents in hot pursuit long enough to meet up with a second car that succeeded in driving Berrigan to a Catholic Worker safe house in New York City.

But our madcap chase triumph was short lived. Not long after his escape from Barton Hall, Berrigan went to visit his customary summer retreat on Block Island, in full knowledge that FBI agents—absurdly posing as birdwatchers—would be waiting for him.

More than forty years after the Freedom Seder in Barton Hall, Rabbi Waskow composed the *Freedom Seder for the Earth* which includes the following verses by his cantor, Linda Hirschhorn written in 2009:

First They Came
©Linda Hirschhorn 2009/2016/2025
(Inspired by Pastor Martin Niemöller)

When first they came for the Communists
I stood by silently, I never was a Communist
What did it matter to me?
What did it matter
What did it matter
What did it matter to me?

Then they came for the Union Men
and I stood silently, I never was a Union Man
What did it matter to me?
What did it matter
What did it matter
What did it matter to me?

Cry out cry out it's still going on today
they're calling your neighbor illegal
they're coming to take her away

And when they came for gays and Jews
I just closed my eyes
I wasn't gay and I wasn't a Jew
so I stood silently by
What did it matter
how could it matter
why should it matter to me?

Cry out cry out it's still going on today
Hispanic, Muslim, a refugee
they're coming to take them away

And now I hear they're coming soon
they're coming soon for me
there's no one left who might cry out
Cry out to set me free

No one of us is truly safe until we all are free
No one of us can truly say it matters not to me
Cry out cry out it's happening this very day
Who is your next door neighbor?
Why have they gone away?

About the Book

In *War Bonds*, Jack Goldman unspools a vivid, tender, and often humorous portrait of a Depression-era Jewish-American boyhood shaped by the competing energies of tradition, rebellion, assimilation, and war. With a keen storyteller's eye, he recounts life among a spirited cast of characters: a tap-dancing father dodging Orthodox expectations, a bar mitzvah faked for family pride, immigrant grandparents clinging to the old ways, and a Los Angeles childhood that veers from near tragedy to unexpected grace.

Goldman's coming-of-age spans the Bronx delicatessens of his youth to the sun-drenched promise of wartime California. Through intimate recollections—both painful and sweet—he captures the strains of poverty, antisemitism, generational conflict, and the enduring power of family improvisation and resilience.

From dice games and candy bribes to jazz saxophone lessons and Christmas trees in Jewish homes, *War Bonds* weaves memory, history, and identity into a deeply personal narrative of survival and belonging. More than a memoir, it is a lyrical meditation on how bonds—between father and son, past and present, war and peace—shape the self. This is a soulful, richly detailed story of growing up American, Jewish, and fiercely human in the 20th century.

About the Author

Born 1934 in Bronx, NY, Jack Goldman graduated from Hollywood High School in 1952. He attended CalTech, thought better of it, and eventually graduated from UCLA. He lived on an Israeli kibbutz, moved to Basel, Switzerland, and worked as a lab tech for Ciba company for two years. He married after returning to Los Angeles, and a Woodrow Wilson fellowship took him to Cornell graduate school in 1968. Goldman dropped out of Cornell to engage in the anti-Vietnam War movement, starting the Glad Day Press and the Dateline Ithaca weekly newsletter. In 1980, he opened The Bookery, a used and antiquarian book. Divorced and remarried in 1982, his daughter was born in 1986. Goldman's son Dan, from his previous marriage, died 2013. Goldman retired in 2020, started writing poetry and his memoirs, and took up chess, for which he thanks Mike Pastore for his encouragement in both endeavors.

www.ingramcontent.com/pod-product-compliance
Lightning Source LLC
Chambersburg PA
CBHW032039290426
44110CB00012B/871